MW01601624

PetsPros Guide to Cat Care for Beginners

Essential Knowledge for First-Time Feline Enthusiasts

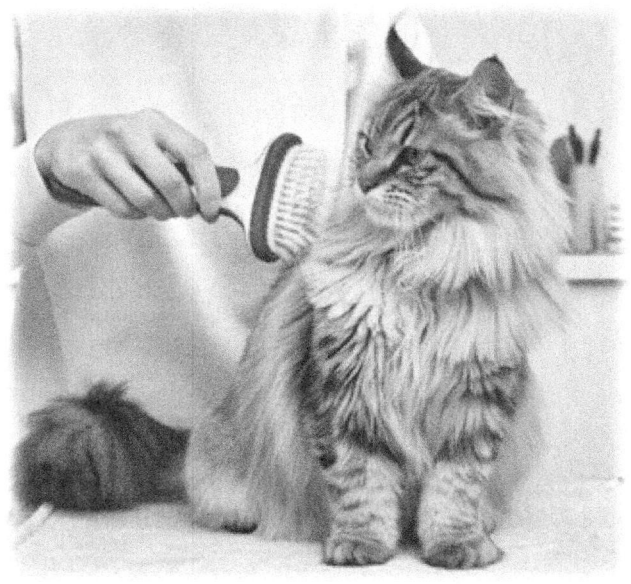

Floyd Camacho

Copyright © 2025 Floyd Camacho

All Rights Reserved

This guide is for informational purposes only. The
author and publisher are not liable for any damages
or injuries resulting from the use of the information
provided. Always consult a professional for specific
advice and follow safety guidelines when
undertaking any such projects.

TABLE OF CONTENTS

INTRODUCTION

Cats have a way of finding a special place in our hearts. One moment, you're watching a cat video online, smiling at their quirky antics. The next, you're standing in a shelter, locking eyes with a tiny, whiskered face, and realizing you're about to bring a new soul into your life. There's something magical about that decision—it's filled with excitement, warmth, and a sense of possibility. You imagine the soft purring as they curl up beside you, the playful pounces on invisible foes, and the quiet companionship during long nights. Owning a cat feels like stepping into a world of gentle affection, where love is exchanged in slow blinks and comforting nudges. But then reality sets in.

That same adorable creature might ignore the fancy bed you bought and instead claim a cardboard box as their throne. They might turn into a relentless 3 AM sprinter, tearing through the house just as you're drifting into sleep. The litter box, which seemed simple enough, somehow becomes a battleground of trial and error. Why won't they use it today? Why do they sometimes stare at you with the judgment of a thousand ancestors? And what about those sudden zoomies, the unexplained meows, the claw marks on your once-pristine couch? These are the moments when new cat owners feel overwhelmed, wondering if they're doing everything right.

It's normal to feel this way. Every cat owner—whether they've had one cat or a dozen—has faced these moments of uncertainty. The truth is, cats are complex creatures with their own personalities, preferences, and peculiarities. Unlike dogs, they don't always offer their affection freely. They require patience, understanding, and a bit of learning on our part. But here's the secret: once you begin to understand them, once you start seeing the world through their eyes, everything changes. That's when the bond between you and your cat truly begins to form.

Knowledge is what turns confusion into confidence. The more you learn about how cats think, how they communicate, and what they need, the more everything starts to make sense. A cat scratching your furniture isn't an act of rebellion; it's an instinct that can be redirected with the right tools. A finicky eater isn't being difficult—they just have preferences, just like we do. Even that mysterious, aloof behavior you might mistake for indifference is often just a different way of expressing love. Cats may not always demand attention the way dogs do, but their affection is deep, sincere, and incredibly rewarding.

This book is here to guide you through it all—the joys, the challenges, and everything in between. It will help you understand what your cat needs to feel safe, happy, and healthy in your home. It will prepare you for the unexpected moments and reassure you that, no matter what, you're not alone in this. Whether you're choosing your first cat, setting up their space, or learning how to interpret their body language, each page will bring you closer to a deeper connection with your feline companion.

The struggles you may face as a cat owner won't last forever. The frustration of a scratched-up couch will fade when you watch your cat stretch contentedly on their new scratching post—the one they actually love this time. The worry of whether they trust you will disappear the moment they curl up in your lap for the first time, their purrs vibrating against your skin. The initial fear of doing something wrong will be replaced by the certainty that you're giving them the best life possible.

No matter where you are in your cat care journey, this book will meet you there. If you're feeling excited, it will fuel that excitement with useful knowledge. If you're feeling uncertain, it will replace that uncertainty with clarity and reassurance. If you're struggling, it will remind you that struggles are just stepping stones toward understanding. And if you're already in love with your cat but want to do better for them, this book will help you take that love and turn it into the best care possible.

Cats have an incredible way of changing our lives. They teach us patience, remind us to find joy in the little things, and show us that love doesn't always need words. In return, they ask for so little—just a safe space, good food, gentle care, and our willingness to understand them. If you're willing to take that step, if you're ready to build a bond that will last for years, you've already started on the right path.

Now, all you have to do is keep going. Turn the page. Let's begin.

.

CHAPTER 1: WHAT IS A CAT? UNDERSTANDING YOUR FELINE COMPANION

A cat is a domesticated carnivorous mammal known for its agility, independence, and sharp hunting instincts. As a companion, it brings both affection and mystery, displaying behaviors that often seem unpredictable.

Understanding what makes a cat unique is essential for proper care and companionship. Its history, breed variations, and body language shape its personality and needs. Recognizing these traits helps in providing a supportive environment, ensuring both physical and emotional well-being. A deeper knowledge of feline characteristics allows for a stronger bond, reducing misunderstandings and improving interactions, making life with a cat more rewarding and harmonious.

The Domestic Cat's Evolution

Cats have been part of human life for thousands of years, yet their journey from wild hunters to beloved pets is fascinating. Unlike dogs, which were domesticated for specific jobs like herding and guarding, cats took a different path. They chose to live alongside humans rather than being bred for a particular purpose. This unique evolution explains many of their behaviors today, from their independent nature to their hunting instincts. Understanding where cats come from helps you appreciate why they act the way they do, making you a better cat owner.

The domestic cat, scientifically known as <u>Felis catus</u>, shares a common ancestor with wildcats from regions like the Middle East and North Africa. The African wildcat (<u>Felis lybica</u>) is the closest relative of today's house cat. Thousands of years ago, early humans stored grain in settlements, attracting rodents. Wildcats, being natural hunters, followed the food source and started living near human communities. Over time, the friendlier and more adaptable cats remained close to humans, while the more aggressive ones stayed wild. This gradual association led to domestication.

Unlike other domesticated animals, cats were never fully controlled by humans. They maintained their ability to hunt and survive on their own, which is why even modern house cats display strong predatory instincts. If you've ever seen your cat chase a toy, stalk a bug, or pounce unexpectedly, that's their inner wildcat at work. Even well-fed indoor cats will instinctively "hunt" because this behavior is deeply embedded in their DNA.

Ancient civilizations played a major role in shaping the relationship between humans and cats. In ancient Egypt, cats were highly valued for their ability to control rat and snake populations. Egyptians even worshipped them, associating them with the goddess Bastet, the deity of protection and fertility. Killing a cat was considered a serious crime. Many Egyptian families kept cats as pets, and when a cat died, it was often mummified and buried with honor. This deep admiration for cats spread to other cultures, reinforcing their role as protectors of homes and food supplies.

In ancient Rome, cats were also appreciated for their pest control skills. They traveled with Roman soldiers, helping to keep grain supplies safe from rodents. As the Roman Empire expanded, so did the presence of domestic cats. They spread to different parts of Europe and Asia, adapting to various climates and lifestyles. However, during the Middle Ages, cats faced a darker period. Superstitions linked them to witchcraft, leading to their persecution. This decline in cat populations may have contributed to the spread of diseases like the Black Plague, as there were fewer cats to control the rodent population.

Despite this, cats survived and regained their place in human society. By the 18th and 19th centuries, they were once again appreciated as both companions and hunters. Selective breeding became more common, leading to the development of various cat breeds with distinct features. While modern domestic cats come in many shapes and sizes, they all share fundamental behaviors inherited from their wild ancestors.

If you observe your cat closely, you'll notice behaviors that link back to their evolutionary history. Kneading with their paws, for example, mimics the movement kittens make while nursing. This instinct remains even in adult cats as a sign of comfort. Similarly, when your cat brings you a dead mouse or toy, they are displaying natural hunting instincts. In the wild, mother cats teach their kittens how to hunt by bringing them prey, and your cat may see you as part of their family.

Understanding your cat's evolution also explains their need for territory and personal space. Wildcats are solitary hunters who establish their own territory. Your house cat carries this trait, which is why they may be picky about where they sleep, eat, and use the litter box. If their environment changes too suddenly, they may become stressed because their instincts tell them to stay in control of their surroundings.

As a cat owner, appreciating this evolutionary background helps you provide a better home for your feline friend. Respect their need for quiet spaces, allow them to hunt in a controlled way (such as playing with interactive toys), and understand that their independence is not a sign of disinterest. Cats are affectionate in their own unique way, often choosing when and how they interact with their human companions.

If you're introducing a cat to a new environment, remember that their instincts may make them cautious at first. Give them time to explore at their own pace rather than forcing interactions. Cats need to feel secure in their surroundings before they can fully settle in.

While cats have come a long way from their wild ancestors, they remain true to their roots. Their evolution has shaped them into intelligent, adaptable, and fascinating creatures. By understanding where they come from, you can build a stronger bond with your cat and create a home that meets their natural needs.

Different Breeds and Their Characteristics

Cats come in all shapes, sizes, and personalities, making them one of the most diverse domesticated animals. While all domestic cats belong to the same species, Felis catus, selective breeding has led to distinct breeds with unique physical traits and temperaments. Understanding different cat breeds can help you choose the right companion for your lifestyle. Some breeds are more social and playful, while others prefer a quiet, independent life. Whether you want a cat that enjoys constant attention or one that prefers occasional affection, knowing the characteristics of different breeds will guide your decision.

There are over 70 recognized cat breeds worldwide, but they all fall into certain broad categories based on their physical features and behaviors. One of the most noticeable distinctions among cat breeds is their coat type. Some have long, luxurious fur that requires daily grooming, while others have short, low-maintenance coats. The Persian cat, for example, is famous for its long, thick fur, which makes it look elegant but also demands regular brushing to prevent matting. On the other hand, the Siamese cat has a short, sleek coat that is much easier to maintain but requires frequent companionship to stay happy.

Hairless cats, such as the Sphynx, are another unique category. While they don't shed like other breeds, they need regular bathing to remove oil buildup on their skin. These cats are known for their affectionate and playful nature, often forming strong bonds with their owners. If you want a cat that enjoys human interaction and isn't shy about demanding attention, a Sphynx might be a great choice. However, if you prefer a more independent cat that doesn't require much hands-on care, a British Shorthair with its plush, dense coat and calm demeanor could be a better fit.

The personality of a cat breed is just as important as its physical traits. Some breeds are naturally active and require plenty of playtime, while others are more relaxed and content to lounge around. Bengal cats, for instance, are highly energetic and need mental stimulation to prevent boredom. They enjoy climbing, playing fetch, and even learning tricks. If you're looking for a low-maintenance lap cat, a Ragdoll might be a better match. These gentle cats are known for their tendency to go limp when picked up, making them one of the most affectionate breeds.

Some breeds are particularly vocal and expressive. The Siamese cat is one of the most talkative breeds, often "conversing" with its owner through loud, distinct meows. If you enjoy a pet that communicates its needs openly, a Siamese cat might be ideal. In contrast, breeds like the Scottish Fold are quieter and more reserved, preferring gentle interactions over constant chatter.

Certain breeds have specific health concerns that potential owners should consider. Purebred cats, due to selective breeding, may be more prone to genetic health issues. Persians, with their flat faces, often suffer from breathing problems and eye infections. Maine Coons, one of the largest domesticated cat breeds, can develop heart conditions if not properly monitored. Knowing these potential health risks allows you to take better care of your cat and choose a breed that matches your ability to provide medical care. Mixed-breed cats, often found in shelters, tend to have fewer genetic health issues and can make wonderful companions.

When selecting a breed, it's important to consider the cat's activity level and social needs. If you live in a small apartment and have a busy schedule, a highly active breed like an Abyssinian might not be the best choice. These cats thrive on interaction and need space to climb and explore. Instead, a British Shorthair or Exotic Shorthair, both known for their easygoing nature, could be more suitable.

Your household environment also plays a role in determining the best breed for you. Some breeds, like the Norwegian Forest Cat, are more suited for cooler climates due to their thick fur. Others, like the Oriental Shorthair, prefer warmer environments. If you have children or other pets, choosing a cat breed with a friendly, tolerant nature is crucial. The Maine Coon is often called the "gentle giant" because of its large size and affectionate personality, making it a great choice for families. In contrast, the Turkish Van is known for its love of water and playful nature but may be too energetic for a household looking for a calmer pet.

Regardless of breed, every cat has its own personality and preferences. While breed characteristics can give you a general idea of what to expect, individual cats may not always fit the typical mold. A Siamese cat might be quiet, or a normally reserved Russian Blue might be unusually playful. It's essential to spend time with a cat before adopting to ensure their personality matches your lifestyle.

Choosing a cat breed isn't just about appearance; it's about finding a companion that fits your daily routine, space, and personal preferences. If you want a playful, interactive cat, breeds like the Abyssinian, Bengal, or Siamese could be great choices. If you prefer a more relaxed companion, a Ragdoll, Scottish Fold, or British Shorthair might be a better fit. If grooming is a concern, short-haired or hairless breeds require less maintenance, while long-haired breeds need regular brushing.

Before adopting a cat, consider your long-term commitment. Some breeds live longer than others, with many cats reaching 15-20 years of age. If you're not prepared for the responsibilities of pet care, including regular vet visits, proper nutrition, and daily interaction, it may be better to wait until you can fully commit to a cat's needs. Each breed has unique requirements, and choosing the right one will ensure a happy relationship between you and your feline friend.

Understanding Cat Behavior and Body Language

Cats are often seen as mysterious creatures because their behavior can be difficult to interpret. Unlike dogs, which are more expressive and social, cats communicate through subtle body language, vocalizations, and actions. Understanding your cat's behavior is key to building a strong bond and ensuring their well-being. Many common feline actions are rooted in instinct, shaped by their evolutionary history. By learning what your cat's signals mean, you can respond appropriately, create a comfortable environment, and strengthen your relationship with your pet.

A cat's tail is one of its most expressive body parts. When a cat holds its tail high, it signals confidence and friendliness. A slightly curved tip can indicate curiosity or excitement, especially when greeting you. If the tail is puffed up like a bottle brush, your cat feels threatened or frightened. This is a defensive response to make themselves appear larger. A twitching or lashing tail usually means irritation or overstimulation, often seen when a cat has had enough petting. If the tail is low and tucked under the body, the cat may be anxious or afraid. Paying attention to these signals helps you understand your cat's mood and respond accordingly.

Ears also reveal a lot about a cat's emotions. When ears are pointed forward, the cat is alert and interested in its surroundings. If they are slightly tilted backward, the cat is unsure or assessing a situation. Flattened ears pressed against the head indicate fear, aggression, or extreme discomfort. This posture is often seen when a cat feels cornered or is in a defensive state. Recognizing these signs allows you to give your cat space when needed and avoid triggering stress or aggression.

A cat's eyes can convey a range of emotions. Slow blinking is a sign of trust and affection. If your cat looks at you and slowly blinks, returning the gesture can reassure them that you feel the same way. Dilated pupils may indicate excitement, playfulness, or fear, depending on the context. If the pupils are very small, it often means the cat is tense, angry, or highly focused. Understanding eye signals helps you gauge your cat's comfort level in different situations.

Cats use their whiskers for more than just sensing their environment. When a cat is relaxed, its whiskers rest naturally on the sides of its face. If they push forward, the cat is curious or excited, often seen when hunting or playing. Whiskers pulled back against the face can indicate fear or aggression. Avoid touching a cat's whiskers unnecessarily, as they are extremely sensitive and play a vital role in spatial awareness.

Vocalization is another way cats communicate. Some breeds, like Siamese cats, are naturally more talkative, while others, like the Russian

Blue, tend to be quieter. A short, high-pitched meow usually signals a greeting or a request for attention. Longer or more drawn-out meows can indicate hunger, frustration, or a demand for something specific. Purring is often associated with contentment, but cats may also purr when in pain or distress to soothe themselves. A growl, hiss, or yowl is a clear warning that the cat feels threatened or wants to be left alone. Understanding your cat's unique vocal patterns helps you respond to their needs appropriately.

Kneading, where a cat presses its paws into a soft surface, is a comforting behavior that originates from kittenhood. Kittens knead their mother's belly to stimulate milk flow, and adult cats continue this behavior when they feel safe and content. If your cat kneads you, it's a sign of trust and affection. Some cats also suckle on blankets or clothing, which can be a leftover habit from kittenhood. While this is usually harmless, excessive kneading or suckling may indicate stress or anxiety.

Scratching is a natural and necessary behavior for cats. It helps them stretch their muscles, sharpen their claws, and mark their territory through scent glands in their paws. Providing scratching posts or pads prevents them from using furniture as a scratching surface. If your cat scratches in unwanted areas, redirect them to an appropriate scratching post and use positive reinforcement when they use it correctly. Trimming their claws regularly can also minimize damage.

Play behavior is deeply connected to a cat's hunting instincts. Even well-fed indoor cats need to "hunt" through play. Toys that mimic prey, such as feather wands or small mice toys, stimulate their natural instincts. Regular play sessions keep your cat physically and mentally active, reducing boredom and destructive behavior. If a cat suddenly stops playing or becomes withdrawn, it may indicate stress or an underlying health issue.

Cats also communicate through grooming. A cat that licks you is showing affection and trust. In multi-cat households, mutual grooming strengthens social bonds. However, excessive grooming or sudden hair loss can be a sign of stress, allergies, or medical conditions. If your cat starts overgrooming, consult a veterinarian to rule out any underlying issues.

Understanding your cat's body language and behavior allows you to create a better living environment for them. If your cat suddenly changes its behavior—becoming unusually aggressive, hiding excessively, or avoiding food—it may be a sign of stress or illness. Cats are experts at hiding discomfort, so any drastic change should be taken seriously. Providing a stable routine, a quiet space, and plenty of enrichment activities helps keep your cat happy and healthy.

Parting Words on Chapter

A cat's unique nature sets it apart from other pets, requiring patience, understanding, and respect for its instincts. Recognizing its behaviors, needs, and traits strengthens the bond between cat and owner, ensuring a fulfilling companionship that benefits both in everyday life.

CHAPTER 2: PREPARING FOR A CAT

Preparing for a cat means creating a safe, comfortable, and well-equipped environment that meets their physical and emotional needs. A new cat requires more than just food and water; they need space, security, and the right resources to thrive. The adjustment period can be challenging, but a well-prepared home ensures a smoother transition. Selecting the right cat, gathering essential supplies, and making necessary adjustments prevent common issues like stress, destructive behavior, or health problems. Understanding what a cat needs before bringing one home helps build a strong foundation for a happy and lasting companionship.

Choosing the Right Cat for Your Home

Bringing a cat into your home is a long-term commitment that should be approached with careful consideration. Cats may be independent by nature, but they still rely on you for food, shelter, healthcare, and companionship. The type of cat you choose will affect your daily routine, your home environment, and even your budget. Whether you are adopting a kitten or an adult cat, selecting the right one will make your journey as a pet owner enjoyable and fulfilling.

There are many factors to consider when choosing a cat, and no two cats are the same. Their breed, temperament, energy level, grooming needs, and health conditions all play a role in determining if they are the right fit for you. Some cats are active and require a lot of playtime, while others are content with lounging around all day. Some breeds shed heavily, while others barely shed at all. Before bringing a cat home, you need to think about your lifestyle, living space, and personal preferences.

A good place to start is deciding between adopting a kitten or an adult cat. Kittens are playful and adorable, but they require more time and patience for training and socialization. They are also more energetic and tend to get into trouble if not supervised. On the other hand, adult cats usually have established personalities, making it easier to predict how they will behave in your home. They may also be litter trained and less destructive than kittens. If you prefer a more predictable and lower-maintenance pet, an adult cat might be the better option.

Another important factor to consider is the breed. While mixed-breed cats are just as loving and wonderful as purebreds, certain breeds have specific traits that may align better with your lifestyle. For example, if you want a cat that is affectionate and enjoys being around people, a Ragdoll or a Maine Coon might be a good choice. If you prefer a cat that is independent and low-maintenance, a British Shorthair or an American Shorthair could be ideal. Siamese cats are highly vocal and social, while Persian cats require daily grooming due to their long fur. Researching different breeds can help you determine which one matches your expectations.

Your living situation is another key aspect to think about. If you live in a small apartment, a highly active breed like a Bengal or an Abyssinian may not be suitable unless you can provide plenty of play opportunities. A quieter breed, such as a Scottish Fold or a Russian Blue, might adapt better to limited space. If you have other pets or children, you'll need a cat that is known for being sociable and patient. Some cats prefer to be the only pet in the household, while others enjoy companionship.

Consider your daily routine as well. If you work long hours and are rarely home, a cat that requires constant attention may not be a good fit. Some cats are more independent and can entertain themselves, while others become anxious or bored when left alone for extended periods. If you have a busy schedule but still want a cat, look for one that is known to be more self-sufficient.

Grooming and maintenance are also essential factors. Long-haired cats, such as Persians and Ragdolls, require frequent brushing to prevent matting and hairballs. If you don't have the time or patience for regular grooming, a short-haired or hairless breed might be a better choice. Shedding can also be a concern, especially if you have allergies. Some breeds, like the Siberian and the Balinese, are considered hypoallergenic because they produce lower levels of allergens. However, no cat is completely hypoallergenic, so if you have severe allergies, spending time around cats before adopting one is a good idea.

Health considerations should not be overlooked. Some breeds are prone to genetic health issues, which may lead to higher veterinary bills over time. For example, Maine Coons and Ragdolls are more susceptible to heart disease, while Persians often suffer from respiratory problems due to their flat faces. If you choose a purebred cat, make sure to get one from a reputable breeder who screens for hereditary conditions. Alternatively, adopting a cat from a shelter or rescue organization can be a great way to give a homeless cat a second chance. Many shelter cats are healthy, loving, and eager to be part of a family.

Before bringing a cat home, it's also important to meet and interact with them. Spend time observing their behavior and personality. Some cats are outgoing and seek attention, while others are more reserved. If a cat is shy or scared, it may take time for them to adjust to a new environment. If you're adopting from a shelter, ask the staff about the cat's history, temperament, and any medical concerns. If you're getting a cat from a breeder, ensure that the kitten or cat has been raised in a clean, loving environment.

Once you have chosen the right cat, make sure your home is ready for their arrival. Have all the essential supplies, including food, water bowls, a litter box, scratching posts, and toys. A comfortable space for them to rest and feel safe is also important. The transition to a new home can be stressful for a cat, so give them time to adjust at their own pace.

Choosing a cat is not just about their looks; it's about finding a pet whose personality, energy level, and needs align with your lifestyle. A well-matched cat can bring years of companionship and joy, while an incompatible choice can lead to frustration for both you and the cat. Take your time, do your research, and make an informed decision.

Bringing a cat into your home is a responsibility that should not be taken lightly. It's tempting to adopt a cat based on appearance, but personality and lifestyle compatibility are far more important. Never choose a cat on impulse, as this can lead to regret and rehoming. Remember that cats can live for 15 to 20 years, so this is a long-term commitment. If you are unsure, spend time with different cats before making a decision.

If you have allergies, visit a household with cats to see how you react before adopting. If you have children, teach them how to interact with a cat respectfully. A cat is not a toy, and rough handling can lead to injuries and behavioral issues. Always adopt from reputable sources and avoid buying from unethical breeders or pet stores that prioritize profit over animal welfare.

Making the right choice will ensure a happy and fulfilling relationship with your feline companion. Take your time, ask questions, and choose a cat that truly fits your home and lifestyle.

Essential Supplies and Equipment

Bringing a cat into your home is an exciting experience, but you must be well-prepared with the right supplies to ensure your feline friend is comfortable, healthy, and happy. Cats are relatively low-maintenance pets compared to dogs, but they still have specific needs that must be met. Having the essential supplies in place before bringing your cat home will make the transition smoother for both of you. From food and litter boxes to scratching posts and carriers, each item plays a role in your cat's well-being.

The most important item you need is high-quality cat food. Cats are obligate carnivores, which means they require a diet primarily composed of meat. Feeding them the right food is crucial for their health. Dry kibble is convenient and helps keep their teeth clean, but wet food provides essential hydration, which is particularly important for cats prone to urinary issues. Some owners prefer a mix of both.

Always choose cat food that contains high levels of animal protein and avoid products with excessive fillers like corn and soy. Fresh water should always be available, preferably in a shallow bowl or a pet fountain, as many cats prefer running water.

A litter box is another essential item. Cats are naturally clean animals and will instinctively use a litter box if it is properly maintained. The size and type of the litter box matter. A larger box gives your cat more space to move comfortably, and covered boxes help contain odors, though some cats prefer open ones. The choice of litter also plays a role in their comfort. Clumping litter makes scooping easier, while non-clumping varieties are more affordable. Some cats are sensitive to scented litters, so it's best to start with an unscented type. The litter box should be placed in a quiet, easily accessible location and cleaned daily to prevent odor buildup and encourage consistent use.

Scratching posts and pads are crucial to protect your furniture. Cats have a natural urge to scratch, which helps them mark their territory, stretch their muscles, and maintain healthy claws. If you don't provide a designated scratching area, your cat will find one—often your couch or carpet. A sturdy scratching post covered in sisal fabric is ideal, as it mimics the texture of tree bark. Some cats prefer horizontal scratching pads, while others like vertical posts. Observing your cat's scratching habits will help you choose the best option.

A comfortable bed provides your cat with a cozy place to rest. While some cats are happy sleeping on furniture or your bed, having a designated cat bed gives them a sense of security. The bed should be soft, warm, and placed in a quiet area of your home. Many cats also enjoy enclosed beds, like cat caves or igloos, which make them feel safe and protected.

Toys are essential for mental and physical stimulation. Cats are natural hunters, and interactive toys help satisfy their instincts. Wand toys with feathers, laser pointers, and small balls keep them entertained and active. Puzzle toys that dispense treats also engage their minds and prevent boredom. Rotating toys regularly keeps things interesting and prevents your cat from losing interest.

A sturdy and secure carrier is a must-have for vet visits and travel. Cats can become stressed when leaving their familiar environment, and a proper carrier ensures their safety. The carrier should be well-ventilated, large enough for your cat to turn around comfortably, and easy to open and close. Hard plastic carriers are more durable and secure, while soft-sided carriers are lightweight and convenient for short trips.

Grooming tools are necessary to keep your cat clean and healthy. A brush or comb suited to your cat's coat type helps prevent matting and reduces shedding. Long-haired cats require daily brushing, while short-haired breeds benefit from weekly grooming. Nail clippers or grinders keep their claws at a manageable length, preventing painful overgrowth. Some cats tolerate having their nails trimmed better than others, so starting this habit early is recommended.

Food and water bowls should be sturdy, shallow, and easy to clean. Stainless steel or ceramic bowls are better than plastic, as they are more hygienic and don't retain odors. Some cats develop "whisker fatigue" when eating from deep bowls, so wide, shallow dishes can make mealtime more comfortable.

A cat tree or climbing structure satisfies a cat's need to climb and observe their surroundings from a high vantage point. It also provides additional scratching surfaces and hiding spots. Cats feel safer when they have elevated areas to retreat to, especially in multi-pet households. If space allows, investing in a cat tree with multiple levels, perches, and cubbies can provide endless entertainment and comfort.

Having a cat-proofed window perch or hammock allows your cat to enjoy the outside world safely. Many cats love watching birds and passersby, and a perch placed near a window provides mental stimulation. If you live in an apartment or high-rise, ensure all windows are secure to prevent accidents.

For multi-cat households, it is important to provide enough resources for each cat. Each cat should have its own litter box, food and water bowls, and resting areas to prevent territorial disputes. Cats can be social, but they also need their own space.

A first aid kit specifically for cats is useful in case of minor injuries or emergencies. Basic supplies include styptic powder for stopping bleeding, antiseptic wipes, tweezers for removing splinters, and a thermometer. Having your vet's contact information and knowing basic first aid techniques can be lifesaving in an emergency.

Once you have gathered all the necessary supplies, introducing them to your cat properly ensures a smooth transition. Allow your cat to explore new items at their own pace, and avoid forcing them to use something they are not yet comfortable with. Providing positive reinforcement, such as treats and praise, encourages them to use their new bed, scratching post, or litter box.

Many new cat owners make the mistake of buying unnecessary items while overlooking essentials. Novelty items like costumes or decorative collars may look cute, but they don't contribute to your cat's well-being. Instead, focus on items that enhance their comfort, health, and happiness.

Be cautious when introducing new products, as some items may not be suitable for every cat. For example, automatic feeders are convenient but may not work well for cats that overeat. Self-cleaning litter boxes are helpful, but some cats are scared of the noise they make. Always observe how your cat reacts to new items before fully incorporating them into their routine.

Investing in high-quality essentials from the start can save you money and trouble in the long run. Cheap products may break easily or be unsafe for your cat. Prioritize your cat's needs, and remember that a happy and well-cared-for cat makes for a loving and loyal companion.

Cat-Proofing Your Home

Bringing a cat into your home means creating a safe and secure environment where they can explore, play, and rest without unnecessary risks. Cats are naturally curious animals, and their instinct to investigate every corner of the house can sometimes lead them into danger. Whether you have a playful kitten or a relaxed adult cat, cat-proofing your home is essential to prevent accidents, injuries, or damage to your belongings. Making a few adjustments to your living space will not only keep your cat safe but also give you peace of mind.

Start by securing all open windows and balconies. Cats love to perch on windowsills and watch the world outside, but an unsecured window poses a serious risk. Even if your cat is not typically adventurous, they might jump or slip out accidentally. Installing sturdy screens or window guards ensures that your cat can enjoy the fresh air safely. If you live in an apartment with a balcony, it's best to keep it off-limits unless it is fully enclosed with cat-proof netting.

Household plants can also be a hidden danger. Some common plants, such as lilies, aloe vera, and pothos, are toxic to cats and can cause serious health issues if ingested. Before bringing a cat home, remove or relocate any toxic plants and replace them with cat-friendly options like spider plants, bamboo palms, or cat grass. If you're unsure about a plant's safety, research it or consult your veterinarian.

Electrical cords and small objects should be kept out of reach. Cats, especially kittens, may be tempted to chew on cords, which can result in electric shocks or choking hazards. Wrapping cords in protective covers, taping them to walls, or using cord organizers can prevent these dangers. Small objects like buttons, rubber bands, hair ties, and paper clips should also be kept away, as they can be easily swallowed and cause blockages.

Cabinets, drawers, and trash bins should be secured, as cats are known to be skilled at opening doors with their paws. Many household items, such as cleaning supplies, detergents, and medications, are toxic to cats. Storing these items in cabinets with childproof locks or high shelves can prevent accidental poisoning. The same applies to trash bins, as cats may dig through garbage and ingest harmful substances. A trash bin with a secure lid will stop your cat from making a mess or eating something unsafe.

Hot surfaces like stovetops and heaters should be off-limits to cats. A curious cat might jump onto a stove that has just been used, leading to burns and serious injuries. When cooking, keep your cat out of the kitchen, and cover the stove with heat-resistant covers when it's not in use. Space heaters should also be placed in areas where your cat cannot knock them over or get too close.

Bathrooms and laundry rooms require extra caution. Always keep the toilet lid closed to prevent your cat from drinking from it or falling in. Cats are also drawn to sinks, bathtubs, and washing machines, so check these areas before using them. Laundry detergents, bleach, and other cleaning agents should be stored in a safe place. Fabric softener sheets, though seemingly harmless, contain chemicals that can be dangerous if chewed or swallowed.

Furniture and sharp objects should be evaluated for safety. Cats love to climb, so unstable bookshelves, wobbly tables, and unsteady decorations should be secured to prevent falls. Sharp objects like scissors, knives, and needles should be stored safely out of reach. If you have glass decorations, fragile vases, or picture frames, consider placing them in cabinets or securing them with adhesive to prevent them from being knocked over.

Certain foods in your kitchen can be toxic to cats. Items like chocolate, onions, garlic, grapes, and caffeine can cause severe health problems. Even small amounts of these foods can be dangerous. Keep all human food stored securely, and never leave food unattended on countertops where your cat can reach it. If you want to offer your cat a treat, stick to vet-approved snacks rather than sharing table scraps.

Cats are natural hunters, and their curiosity can lead them into places they shouldn't be. Household appliances such as refrigerators, dryers, dishwashers, and ovens can become unexpected hiding spots. Before using these appliances, always check inside to make sure your cat hasn't snuck in. Keeping the doors of these appliances closed when not in use can prevent accidents.

Toys and scratching posts can help redirect your cat's energy away from household items. Cats may chew on inappropriate objects if they are bored or teething. Providing safe, interactive toys keeps them occupied and less likely to explore dangerous items. Scratching posts help prevent them from damaging furniture, so place them in areas where your cat likes to scratch.

If you have multiple pets, make sure your cat has a safe space to retreat to. Some cats enjoy the company of other animals, while others prefer solitude. Creating a designated area for your cat, whether it's a quiet room, a cozy bed, or a perch, allows them to feel secure and relaxed. Cats also enjoy vertical spaces, so cat trees, shelves, or window perches can help them escape from stressful situations.

Taking the time to cat-proof your home will prevent accidents and create a safe space where your cat can thrive. Many common household items that seem harmless to humans can pose a danger to cats, so staying mindful of potential risks is essential. Once your home is properly set up, your cat will have a secure and enjoyable environment to explore.

Leaving dangerous items within your cat's reach can lead to life-threatening situations. Always check your home for potential hazards, and make adjustments as needed. Cats are fast learners, but they don't always recognize what is safe and what isn't. Supervise them during their first few days in a new home to see how they interact with their surroundings.

Never underestimate your cat's ability to find hidden dangers. Even if you think an object is out of reach, your cat might surprise you. Stay proactive about their safety, and regularly reassess your home for new risks. A well-cat-proofed home will keep your feline friend safe, happy, and out of trouble.

Parting Words on Chapter

A well-prepared home sets the stage for a positive experience with a new cat. Ignoring small details can lead to long-term issues. Gradual introductions, consistent routines, and patience help ease the transition, ensuring your cat feels secure and adapts comfortably.

CHAPTER 3: SETTING UP YOUR CAT'S LIVING SPACE

A cat's living space is the environment where it eats, sleeps, plays, and feels secure. Comfort and accessibility in this space directly affect health, behavior, and overall well-being. A well-organized home with designated areas for rest, activity, and hygiene prevents stress and destructive habits. Properly placed furniture, litter boxes, and climbing structures encourage natural instincts while maintaining cleanliness. Attention to temperature, lighting, and scent ensures a welcoming atmosphere. Creating an enriched environment with scratching posts, perches, and cozy retreats strengthens the bond between pet and owner, making daily life smoother and more enjoyable for both.

Creating a Comfortable Environment

Bringing a cat into your home is more than just providing food and water. Your cat needs a space where it feels safe, relaxed, and happy. A comfortable environment is essential for both its physical and mental well-being. Cats are naturally territorial animals, meaning they like to have control over their surroundings. When their environment is stressful or uncomfortable, they can develop behavioral issues, anxiety, or even health problems. By setting up your home in a way that suits your cat's needs, you create a peaceful and loving space where it can thrive.

Your cat's comfort starts with space. It doesn't matter if you live in a large house or a small apartment—what matters is how you arrange it. Cats need areas to explore, hide, rest, and play. If you have a kitten, it may take some time for it to get used to the new environment. Adult cats, especially those adopted from shelters, might need even more patience as they adjust. You should prepare a specific area for your cat before bringing it home. A quiet corner with a soft bed, some toys, and access to food and water is a great start. Make sure this space is not near loud noises, such as a television, washing machine, or a busy entrance. Cats prefer calm, predictable surroundings.

Temperature plays a big role in your cat's comfort. Cats love warmth. They often seek out sunny spots or cozy blankets. If your home is cold, you should provide extra warmth with soft bedding, heated pads, or even a cat-friendly spot near a radiator. On hot days, ensure that your cat has a cool place to retreat to, such as a shaded area or a well-ventilated room. Hydration is also important, so always provide fresh water, especially during warm weather.

Lighting also affects your cat's comfort. Natural light is ideal because it helps regulate their sleep cycle and mood. If your home doesn't get much sunlight, consider using soft, warm lighting instead of harsh, bright lights. Cats are crepuscular animals, meaning they are most active during dawn and dusk. Having dim lighting during these times mimics their natural environment and makes them feel more at ease.

Another important factor is noise level. Cats have very sensitive hearing and can get stressed by loud or sudden noises. If you have a noisy household, create a quiet sanctuary for your cat where it can escape when it feels overwhelmed. Avoid playing loud music near your cat's resting area. If you have children or other pets, teach them to respect your cat's need for quiet time.

Scent is another element that contributes to a comfortable environment. Cats have a strong sense of smell and use scents to feel secure. When bringing a new cat home, try using familiar scents, like a blanket from its previous home or an item that smells like you. If your cat rubs against furniture, it's marking its territory with scent glands. This behavior helps it feel more at home, so allow it to do so. Using calming pheromone sprays can also help if your cat seems anxious.

Furniture arrangement is another detail to consider. Cats enjoy high places where they can observe their surroundings. If you don't have tall furniture, consider installing wall-mounted shelves or a cat tree. Having elevated spaces gives your cat a sense of security. At the same time, make sure it has access to cozy, enclosed spaces like small beds, cardboard boxes, or cat tunnels. These provide a safe retreat when your cat wants privacy.

Your cat's environment should also be enriched with activities to keep it mentally stimulated. A bored cat can become destructive or depressed. Provide scratching posts, interactive toys, and opportunities for climbing. Playing with your cat daily strengthens your bond and prevents behavioral issues. Puzzle feeders are also a great way to keep your cat entertained while encouraging natural hunting instincts.

Cleanliness is a crucial part of a comfortable environment. Cats are very clean animals, and they feel uneasy in a dirty space. Regularly clean your cat's bedding, litter box, and food and water bowls. Avoid using strong-smelling cleaning products, as cats are sensitive to chemical scents. Use mild, pet-friendly cleaners to ensure their space remains fresh without overwhelming their senses.

A stable routine also contributes to comfort. Cats love predictability. Try to feed your cat at the same times every day and avoid making sudden changes in their environment. If you must rearrange furniture, introduce the changes gradually so your cat has time to adjust. If you're bringing in a new pet, do so slowly and carefully to prevent stress.

Providing a comfortable environment is an ongoing process. As your cat grows or ages, its needs may change. Pay attention to its behavior and adjust its surroundings accordingly. A young, active cat may need more play areas, while an older cat may appreciate softer bedding and easier access to its favorite spots.

Your cat depends on you to create a safe and happy home. Be patient and observant, and always make adjustments based on your cat's comfort. If your cat shows signs of stress—such as hiding excessively, avoiding certain areas, or acting aggressively—it may not feel secure in its environment. In such cases, reassess the space and try to identify what might be causing discomfort.

A happy and comfortable cat is a healthy cat. By taking the time to create a space that meets its needs, you ensure a loving, stress-free environment for your furry companion.

Litter Box Basics

A litter box is one of the most important parts of your cat's daily life. It is not just a place for your cat to relieve itself but also a crucial element in maintaining hygiene and preventing unwanted accidents in your home. A well-maintained litter box ensures your cat feels safe and comfortable while also making it easier for you to manage waste. Choosing the right type of litter box, placing it correctly, keeping it clean, and understanding your cat's preferences all play a role in making litter training successful.

Selecting the right litter box is the first step. There are different types, including open trays, covered boxes, self-cleaning models, and top-entry designs. Each cat has its own preference, so you may need to experiment to see which one works best. Open trays are simple and allow easy access, but they can let odors spread. Covered boxes offer privacy and contain smells, but some cats dislike feeling trapped inside. Self-cleaning litter boxes are convenient for owners but may be too noisy for sensitive cats. The size of the litter box also matters. It should be at least 1.5 times the length of your cat, allowing it enough space to turn around comfortably.

Choosing the right litter is just as important. There are many types, including clumping clay, non-clumping clay, silica gel crystals, recycled paper, and natural options like wood pellets or corn-based litter. Clumping clay is the most popular because it forms solid clumps that are easy to scoop. However, some cats may have respiratory sensitivities to the dust it produces. Non-clumping litter absorbs moisture but requires frequent full changes. Silica gel litter controls odor well but may feel strange on your cat's paws. Natural litters are eco-friendly but may not always control odors as effectively. The best way to find the right litter is to observe your cat's reaction. If it avoids the litter box, it might not like the texture or smell of the litter.

Placement of the litter box significantly affects whether your cat will use it consistently. The box should be in a quiet, accessible location where your cat feels safe. Avoid placing it near noisy appliances like washing machines or in high-traffic areas where your cat may feel exposed. If you have multiple cats, you should have one litter box per cat plus an extra one. This prevents territorial issues and ensures that no cat has to wait to use the litter box. Never place the litter box near food and water bowls, as cats naturally avoid eliminating near their eating areas.

Cleaning the litter box regularly is crucial for your cat's hygiene and comfort. Cats are very clean animals, and a dirty litter box may cause them to avoid using it altogether. Scoop out waste at least once or twice a day to keep the box fresh. A complete litter change should be done once a week or as needed, depending on the type of litter you use. When cleaning the box, use mild soap and warm water instead of strong-smelling disinfectants like bleach or ammonia, as these scents can deter your cat.

Litter training is usually easy since cats instinctively bury their waste. If you have a kitten, introduce it to the litter box as soon as you bring it home. Place the kitten in the box after meals and naps, gently guiding it to dig. Most kittens catch on quickly. For an older cat that is new to your home, patience is key. If the cat does not use the litter box, try different types of litter or adjust the box's location. Never punish a cat for accidents, as this will only create stress and make the problem worse.

If your cat suddenly stops using the litter box, there could be an underlying issue. Medical conditions like urinary tract infections, kidney problems, or digestive issues can cause litter box avoidance. Stress, household changes, or conflicts with other pets can also contribute. If your cat starts urinating outside the box, observe if there are other symptoms like frequent trips to the box, straining, or crying while urinating. In such cases, consult a veterinarian immediately.

Some cats develop preferences for certain textures or locations when eliminating. If your cat starts using carpets or corners of the house, try using a litter box in that spot temporarily before gradually moving it to a more suitable location. Enzyme-based cleaners should be used to remove odors from inappropriate elimination areas, as regular cleaning products may not completely eliminate the scent, which can encourage repeat accidents.

Once your cat is fully accustomed to using the litter box, maintaining a consistent routine is important. Avoid sudden changes in the type of litter or location of the box, as this can confuse your cat. If you need to change the litter type, mix the new and old litter gradually over a week to help your cat adjust.

Your cat's comfort with its litter box depends on cleanliness, accessibility, and the right choice of litter. Ignoring any of these factors can result in undesirable behaviors like elimination outside the box. If you notice persistent litter box issues, address them quickly to avoid long-term habits that are difficult to break. Keeping your cat's litter box clean and well-maintained benefits both your cat's health and your home's cleanliness.

Cat Furniture and Climbing Structures

Cats are natural climbers, scratchers, and explorers. In the wild, they climb trees to observe their surroundings, escape danger, and find a secure place to rest. Even as domesticated pets, these instincts remain strong. Providing cat furniture and climbing structures helps satisfy these natural behaviors while also keeping your home and furniture safe from damage. Without appropriate outlets, cats may resort to scratching sofas, jumping onto fragile shelves, or knocking over household items. By offering the right structures, you create an environment that keeps your cat happy, active, and engaged.

Cat trees are one of the most important pieces of furniture for indoor cats. These multi-level structures provide various platforms for climbing, scratching, and resting. Some cat trees include enclosed spaces for hiding, which help anxious cats feel secure. Others have hammocks or perches that allow cats to lounge while observing their environment. When choosing a cat tree, consider its height and stability. A taller cat tree offers more opportunities for exercise and exploration, but it should be sturdy enough to prevent wobbling. A base that is too narrow or lightweight can cause the structure to tip over, making your cat reluctant to use it. If you have multiple cats, a larger cat tree with multiple levels and hideouts can help prevent territorial disputes.

Wall-mounted shelves and perches are excellent alternatives for smaller spaces. These structures mimic the natural climbing experience of trees, allowing cats to move vertically rather than just across the floor. Wall-mounted cat furniture can be arranged in different ways to create a fun and challenging climbing course. You can install steps that lead to a high perch where your cat can relax undisturbed. Make sure the shelves are securely attached to the wall to support your cat's weight. Placing them near a window gives your cat an interesting view, making the space even more appealing.

Scratching posts are essential to protect your furniture while keeping your cat's claws healthy. Cats scratch to mark territory, stretch their muscles, and shed old claw layers. If they don't have a designated scratching area, they will find other surfaces to use, such as couches, carpets, or door frames. A good scratching post should be tall enough for your cat to stretch fully. The material also matters—sisal rope is a popular choice because it provides the right texture for scratching, while cardboard and carpeted posts work well for some cats. Place the scratching post in a spot your cat frequents, preferably near its favorite resting place. If your cat ignores it, try sprinkling catnip on the post or using a toy to encourage interaction.

Window perches give your cat a comfortable place to relax while observing the outside world. Many cats enjoy watching birds, people, and passing cars, which provides mental stimulation. A window perch can be attached to a windowsill or mounted with suction cups on the glass. Ensure that the perch is strong enough to support your cat's weight. Some models come with soft cushions for added comfort. If your home has limited space, a window perch is a great way to provide vertical territory without taking up floor space.

Tunnels and hiding spots cater to a cat's need for security and play. In the wild, cats seek out hidden areas for resting and protection. Providing cozy hiding spaces, such as enclosed beds, covered cat condos, or collapsible fabric tunnels, allows your cat to retreat when it feels overwhelmed. Tunnels also encourage play, especially for energetic kittens or multi-cat households. Placing a tunnel near other cat furniture, like a scratching post or cat tree, creates an engaging play area where your cat can climb, hide, and pounce.

Placement of cat furniture matters just as much as the type of furniture itself. If the furniture is in an area your cat rarely visits, it may not use it. Position cat trees and shelves in places where your cat naturally spends time. If your cat enjoys climbing onto bookshelves or countertops, consider placing a cat tree nearby to offer a better alternative. If your cat scratches the corner of your couch, placing a scratching post next to it can redirect the behavior. Encouraging use may take some time, but with patience and the right positioning, your cat will gradually adapt.

Regular maintenance of cat furniture is necessary to keep it in good condition. Scratching posts wear out over time, and the material may need to be replaced. Vacuuming cat trees and perches removes fur and dust, keeping the space clean and comfortable. If your cat loses interest in a particular structure, rearranging its position or adding toys can renew its curiosity. Some cat furniture allows you to swap out old parts, such as replacing worn-out scratching surfaces or changing cushion covers.

A well-equipped home with cat-friendly furniture reduces stress and prevents destructive behavior. It also provides a sense of security, especially for cats that tend to be anxious or territorial. Investing in quality cat furniture ensures your pet has a stimulating and comfortable environment, making it less likely to develop behavioral issues. Providing climbing structures, scratching posts, and cozy resting spots supports both physical health and mental well-being, leading to a happier and more content cat.

Parting Words on Chapter

A cat thrives in a space designed to meet its needs for comfort, security, and activity. Attention to detail in setup prevents behavioral issues and promotes well-being. Regular adjustments based on observation ensure the environment remains engaging and suitable as needs evolve.

CHAPTER 4: FEEDING YOUR CAT

Feeding is the foundation of a cat's health, influencing energy levels, growth, and overall well-being. A balanced diet provides essential nutrients, supports organ function, and prevents common health issues such as obesity and malnutrition. Proper feeding practices ensure a cat maintains a healthy weight, strong immune system, and a shiny coat. Understanding dietary needs, portion control, and meal frequency helps create a structured routine that meets nutritional requirements without overfeeding. Selecting appropriate treats and supplements enhances health without disrupting a balanced diet. Establishing good feeding habits promotes longevity, reduces the risk of disease, and keeps a cat active and content.

Choosing the Right Diet

Cats are unique creatures with specific dietary needs that differ from other pets. Unlike dogs, they are obligate carnivores, meaning their bodies are designed to process meat as their primary food source. Choosing the right diet for your cat is crucial for their overall health, lifespan, and well-being. The food you provide will affect their energy levels, coat condition, digestive health, and even their behavior.

Many new cat owners assume that any pet food labeled for cats is good enough, but this isn't always true. There are many factors to consider, including nutritional content, food quality, feeding preferences, and specific health conditions. You need to balance protein, fat, vitamins, and minerals while avoiding unnecessary fillers or harmful ingredients. Understanding what goes into your cat's food will help you make better decisions and keep your furry friend happy and healthy.

Understanding Your Cat's Nutritional Needs

Cats require a high-protein, low-carbohydrate diet because their bodies rely on protein as their primary energy source. Unlike humans and dogs, they do not efficiently process carbohydrates, which means grain-heavy diets can lead to weight gain and health issues. The essential nutrients in a cat's diet include:

Protein – This is the most important nutrient in a cat's diet. It supports muscle growth, tissue repair, and energy. Look for high-quality protein sources like chicken, turkey, beef, fish, or lamb.

Taurine – This is an essential amino acid that cats must get from their diet. It is found in animal-based proteins and is necessary for heart function, vision, and overall health.

Fats – Healthy fats, such as omega-3 and omega-6 fatty acids, are essential for brain function, skin health, and a shiny coat.

Vitamins and Minerals – Cats need a well-balanced intake of vitamins like A, D, E, and B-complex, as well as minerals like calcium and phosphorus for strong bones and teeth.

Water – Hydration is key. Unlike dogs, cats don't always feel thirsty even when they need water, so their diet should include moisture-rich foods.

Types of Cat Food

There are different types of cat food available, and choosing the right one depends on your cat's health, age, and preferences.

Dry Food (Kibble) – This is the most convenient and affordable option. It has a long shelf life and helps keep your cat's teeth clean by reducing plaque buildup. However, it has lower moisture content, so it is important to provide enough water to keep your cat hydrated. Look for high-protein kibble with real meat as the first ingredient. Avoid brands that use corn, wheat, or soy as fillers.

Wet Food (Canned Food) – This type of food contains high moisture levels, which helps prevent dehydration and supports kidney function. It is often more palatable for cats and is closer to their natural diet. Wet food is recommended for cats with urinary tract issues or older cats that struggle to chew dry food. However, it is more expensive and spoils faster than kibble.

Raw Food Diet – Some cat owners prefer a raw or homemade diet to mimic what cats would eat in the wild. This includes raw meats, organs, and bones. While this diet can be beneficial, it requires careful preparation to ensure your cat gets all the necessary nutrients. There is also a risk of bacterial contamination if the food isn't handled properly. If you choose this option, consult a vet to ensure a balanced diet.

Semi-Moist Food – This is less common but available in some stores. It is soft and chewy, often shaped like small meat pieces. While convenient, it often contains artificial colors, preservatives, and high levels of sugar or salt, which aren't ideal for cats.

Choosing the Right Food for Your Cat

When selecting the best food for your cat, consider these factors:

Age – Kittens, adult cats, and senior cats have different nutritional needs. Kittens require high protein and fat for growth, while seniors may need diets tailored for joint health and weight management.

Activity Level – Active cats need more calories, while indoor or overweight cats require a controlled diet to prevent obesity.

Health Conditions – Some cats have specific dietary needs due to allergies, kidney disease, diabetes, or digestive problems. Special prescription diets may be necessary.

Ingredients List – Always check the ingredients list before purchasing cat food. Look for whole meat sources rather than meat by-products. Avoid artificial additives, excessive grains, and unnecessary fillers.

Brand Reputation – Choose reputable brands known for quality control and balanced nutrition. Some cheaper brands cut corners, using low-quality ingredients that could harm your cat over time.

Common Mistakes to Avoid

Many cat owners make mistakes when choosing food, leading to health problems:

Feeding only dry food – While kibble is convenient, relying solely on dry food can lead to dehydration and kidney issues.

Ignoring food allergies – If your cat develops itchy skin, vomiting, or diarrhea, it might be an allergic reaction to an ingredient in their food.

Overfeeding or underfeeding – Following portion recommendations is essential to maintaining a healthy weight.

Switching diets too quickly – If you need to change your cat's food, do it gradually over 7–10 days to avoid digestive upset.

Ensuring a Healthy Diet for Your Cat

Choosing the right diet is one of the most important responsibilities of a cat owner. It affects every aspect of your cat's life, from energy levels to long-term health. A well-balanced diet, rich in protein and essential nutrients, will help your cat thrive.

When introducing a new food, observe your cat's reaction. If they refuse to eat or experience digestive issues, reconsider the choice. Never feed your cat human food like chocolate, onions, garlic, or dairy products, as these can be toxic.

If you're unsure about what diet is best for your cat, consult a veterinarian. Every cat is unique, and a professional can recommend the best diet plan based on your pet's age, weight, and health condition. Making the right dietary choices now

will contribute to a longer, happier life for your
cat.

How Much and How Often to Feed Your Cat

Feeding your cat the right amount of food at the right time is just as important as choosing the right diet. Overfeeding can lead to obesity, diabetes, and other health problems, while underfeeding can cause malnutrition, weakness, and behavioral issues. Many cat owners struggle to find the right balance, especially since every cat has different needs based on age, activity level, metabolism, and overall health. Understanding portion sizes and meal schedules will help you keep your cat healthy and maintain a consistent feeding routine.

Cats are creatures of habit, and their eating schedule should reflect their natural instincts. In the wild, cats hunt multiple small prey throughout the day, rather than eating large meals at once. This means that their digestive system is built for small, frequent meals rather than one or two big portions. Replicating this natural feeding pattern can prevent digestive issues, help maintain energy levels, and reduce begging behaviors.

Determining the Right Amount of Food

There is no universal rule for how much to feed your cat because their dietary needs vary based on different factors. The most important consideration is caloric intake rather than just portion size. Cats need a specific number of calories per day, which can be calculated based on their weight, age, and activity level.

On average, an adult cat requires 20 to 30 calories per pound of body weight per day. This means a 10-pound cat typically needs between 200 and 300 calories daily. However, this number can change if your cat is more active, less active, or has specific health needs. Kittens, for example, require more calories per pound because they are growing, while senior cats may need fewer calories to avoid weight gain.

The food packaging usually provides feeding guidelines based on weight, but these are general recommendations. If your cat is gaining or losing weight unexpectedly, you may need to adjust their portions accordingly. A veterinarian can help determine the exact calorie requirement based on your cat's body condition.

Meal Frequency Based on Age and Lifestyle

Kittens need frequent feeding since they grow rapidly and burn energy quickly. For the first few weeks, they rely entirely on their mother's milk or a formula if they are orphaned. By four to six weeks old, they can start eating solid food along with milk.

From eight weeks to six months, kittens should be fed three to four times a day with nutrient-rich food that supports their development. Their small stomachs require frequent meals to ensure steady energy levels. By six months to one year, their metabolism starts to slow, and you can transition to two to three meals a day.

Adult cats typically thrive on two meals per day, one in the morning and one in the evening. This schedule aligns well with their natural hunting instincts and provides consistent energy levels throughout the day. Some cats prefer smaller, more frequent meals, and if that suits their eating behavior, three meals per day can be an option.

Senior cats (aged seven and above) may require more tailored feeding schedules based on their health and mobility. Some older cats develop joint problems or slower metabolism, making weight management a priority. Others may develop kidney disease or dental issues, which means they might prefer softer food or need smaller, more frequent meals to stay comfortable.

Indoor cats generally have a more sedentary lifestyle, meaning they require fewer calories compared to outdoor or highly active cats. If your cat spends most of the day lounging, portion control is necessary to prevent obesity.

Outdoor cats, on the other hand, may require higher calorie intake due to increased physical activity.

Free-Feeding vs. Scheduled Feeding

Some cat owners opt for free-feeding, where dry food is left out all day, allowing the cat to eat whenever they feel hungry. While this method provides convenience, it can lead to overeating and obesity, especially in indoor cats that do not burn as many calories. Additionally, free-feeding does not work well with wet food, as it spoils quickly.

Scheduled feeding is the preferred method for most cats. It allows for better portion control and ensures that your cat is eating a balanced diet rather than snacking all day. Scheduled feeding also helps establish a routine, making it easier to monitor appetite changes, which can be an early sign of illness.

If you use a combination of wet and dry food, you can schedule wet meals at fixed times while leaving a measured amount of dry food available for snacking. However, if your cat tends to overeat, it's best to stick to meal times and remove uneaten food after 30 minutes.

Recognizing Signs of Overfeeding and Underfeeding

A cat that is overfed may gain excessive weight, become less active, and have difficulty grooming. Obesity can lead to serious health problems such as diabetes, arthritis, and liver disease. If you notice that your cat's ribs are difficult to feel under a thick layer of fat, or if they have a round belly with little waist definition, it may be time to reduce portion sizes and increase exercise.

An underfed cat, on the other hand, may appear thin, have low energy, and beg for food constantly. If you notice visible ribs, a protruding spine, or dull fur, your cat may not be getting enough nutrients. Rapid weight loss is especially dangerous in cats because it can lead to hepatic lipidosis, a life-threatening liver disease. If your cat seems underweight despite eating, consult a veterinarian to rule out medical conditions.

Creating a Healthy Feeding Routine

Establishing a regular feeding schedule helps keep your cat's metabolism stable and prevents behavioral problems. Cats thrive on routine, so feeding them at the same time every day creates a sense of security. Avoid sudden changes in meal times, as this can lead to stress and food aggression.

Always provide fresh water alongside meals, as dehydration can lead to kidney problems and urinary tract infections. If your cat prefers running water, consider a cat water fountain to encourage better hydration.

Avoid giving your cat human food, as many ingredients are toxic to felines. Onions, garlic, chocolate, caffeine, alcohol, and dairy products should never be given to cats. Even small amounts of these foods can cause serious health issues.

If you need to switch your cat's diet, do so gradually over seven to ten days to avoid digestive upset. Mix the new food with the old food in increasing amounts each day until the transition is complete. This method helps your cat adjust to the new food without stress.

Monitoring your cat's weight and body condition regularly will help you determine if adjustments are needed. If you're unsure about portion sizes or meal frequency, your veterinarian can provide personalized guidance. Feeding your cat correctly will ensure they stay healthy, active, and happy for years to come.

Treats and Supplements

Treats and supplements can play an important role in your cat's diet when used correctly. Treats are a great way to reward good behavior, build a bond with your cat, and provide enrichment. However, giving too many treats can lead to weight gain and an unbalanced diet. Supplements, on the other hand, are used to support your cat's overall health, but they should only be given when necessary. Understanding how to incorporate treats and supplements into your cat's routine can help ensure their long-term health and happiness.

Many cat owners make the mistake of thinking that all treats are harmless or that supplements are always beneficial. In reality, both should be chosen carefully and used in moderation. Overfeeding treats can lead to obesity, while unnecessary supplements can cause imbalances in your cat's body. Choosing the right treats and knowing when to use supplements will help you keep your cat healthy without unintended negative effects.

Choosing the Right Treats for Your Cat

Cats love treats, and they can be useful for training, rewarding good behavior, or simply making your cat feel loved. However, not all treats are created equal. Many commercial treats contain high levels of artificial additives, sugar, and unhealthy fillers that can contribute to weight gain or digestive issues.

When selecting treats, always check the ingredient list. Look for treats made from high-quality proteins such as chicken, salmon, or turkey. Avoid products with excessive carbohydrates, grains, or artificial colors. Treats should ideally be low in calories to prevent unwanted weight gain. If you are unsure about a particular brand, consult your veterinarian.

It's important to remember that treats should never replace a balanced diet. Cats rely on their regular meals for essential nutrients, and treats should only make up about 10% or less of their daily caloric intake. Giving too many treats can lead to a cat refusing their regular food, which can result in nutritional deficiencies over time.

Some of the best treat options include freeze-dried meat, small portions of cooked fish or chicken, and catnip-infused treats. Freeze-dried treats are a great choice because they retain most of their natural nutrients and do not contain artificial preservatives. If you prepare homemade treats, always ensure they are free from seasonings, onions, garlic, or other toxic ingredients.

Understanding Supplements and When to Use Them

Unlike treats, supplements are designed to support specific aspects of your cat's health, such as joint function, digestion, or skin and coat health. However, most cats on a well-balanced commercial diet do not need additional supplements unless recommended by a vet. Over-supplementation can cause health problems, so it's important to understand which supplements are necessary and which are not.

Taurine is one of the most essential nutrients for cats, as it supports heart health, vision, and overall well-being. Fortunately, commercial cat foods are formulated to contain the correct amount of taurine, so additional supplementation is usually unnecessary. However, if you are feeding a homemade or raw diet, you may need to add taurine to prevent deficiencies.

Omega-3 and Omega-6 fatty acids are beneficial for skin and coat health. Cats with dry skin, excessive shedding, or dull fur may benefit from fish oil or flaxseed oil supplements. These healthy fats also support brain function and can help reduce inflammation, particularly in cats with arthritis or allergies.

Probiotics can help maintain a healthy digestive system. Cats with sensitive stomachs, diarrhea, or recent antibiotic use may benefit from probiotic supplements. These supplements introduce beneficial bacteria into the gut, helping to balance digestion and improve nutrient absorption.

Glucosamine and chondroitin are common supplements for joint health, particularly in older cats. If your cat has arthritis, stiffness, or difficulty jumping, these supplements may help improve mobility. While they are generally safe, they should only be given under veterinary supervision to ensure the correct dosage.

Multivitamins are not necessary for most cats that eat a high-quality diet. Giving too many vitamins, especially fat-soluble ones like Vitamin A and D, can lead to toxicity. Before giving a multivitamin, consult your veterinarian to determine whether your cat truly needs additional nutrients.

Treats and Supplements for Special Conditions

Certain health conditions may require special dietary adjustments, including the use of specific treats and supplements. For instance, overweight cats should receive low-calorie treats such as freeze-dried meat or small pieces of cooked fish. Avoid high-fat treats, as they can contribute to further weight gain.

Cats with kidney disease often require low-phosphorus diets, so it's important to choose treats that align with their dietary restrictions. Avoid cheese, dairy, and high-protein treats unless approved by your vet.

If your cat has food allergies or sensitivities, opt for limited-ingredient treats. Hypoallergenic treats made from novel proteins like duck or venison can help prevent allergic reactions. Always monitor your cat's response to new treats and discontinue any that cause digestive upset or itching.

Dental treats can be beneficial for oral hygiene, especially for cats prone to tartar buildup or gum disease. Some specially formulated dental treats help scrape plaque off the teeth, reducing the risk of dental problems. However, dental treats should never replace regular dental care, such as brushing or professional cleanings.

Moderation and Safe Practices

It's easy to get carried away with treats, especially when your cat begs for more. However, overfeeding treats can lead to obesity, picky eating habits, and digestive issues. To prevent these problems, set a daily limit on treats and stick to it. If your cat starts rejecting their regular food in favor of treats, reduce treat frequency and encourage proper meal habits.

When using supplements, always follow the recommended dosage. Too much of any supplement can have negative effects on your cat's health. If you're considering adding a new supplement to your cat's diet, consult your veterinarian to ensure it's appropriate.

Never give your cat human supplements or medications without professional guidance. Some human vitamins and minerals are toxic to cats, even in small amounts. For example, iron and certain essential oils can be harmful or even fatal if ingested.

Store treats and supplements in a cool, dry place to maintain their freshness. Expired or spoiled treats can cause food poisoning, leading to vomiting or diarrhea. If you notice any changes in the smell, texture, or color of a treat, discard it immediately.

Keeping treats and supplements under control will help ensure that your cat receives only the nutrients they truly need. While treats are a great way to show affection, they should not compromise a balanced diet. Supplements should always be used with a purpose, not just as an extra addition to an already complete diet. With careful selection and moderation, you can keep your cat healthy while still indulging them in small, enjoyable rewards.

Parting Words on Chapter

A cat's diet shapes its health, energy, and longevity. Feeding correctly prevents common health issues and strengthens the bond between owner and pet. Consistency in meals, portion control, and selecting quality food ensure optimal nutrition, keeping a cat active, happy, and well-nourished.

CHAPTER 5: CAT HEALTH BASICS

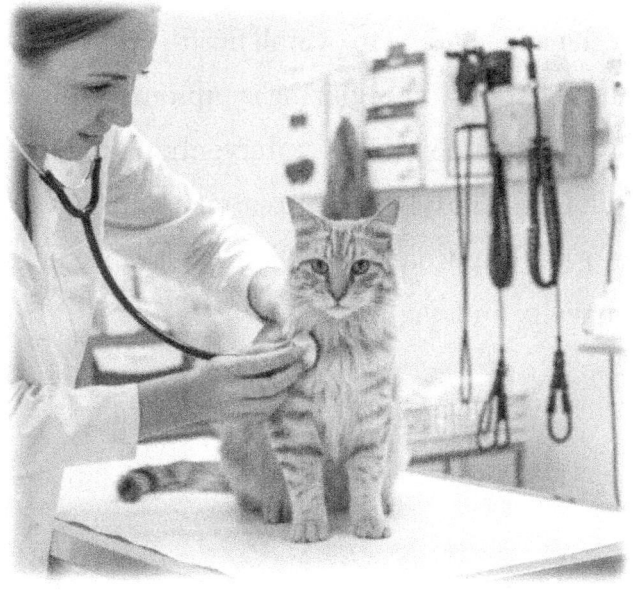

Cat health refers to the overall physical and medical well-being of a feline, encompassing routine care, disease prevention, and early detection of illnesses. Understanding basic health principles ensures a longer, more comfortable life for a pet. Regular veterinary visits, vaccinations, and preventative measures protect against common diseases and medical emergencies. Cats are skilled at hiding discomfort, making proactive care essential. Proper nutrition, parasite control, and dental hygiene contribute to overall health and prevent complications. Recognizing symptoms of illness early allows for timely intervention, reducing suffering and costly treatments. A well-informed approach to feline health promotes longevity and quality of life.

Understanding Routine Vet Visits

Taking your cat to the vet for regular checkups is one of the most important things you can do to keep them healthy. Many cat owners only visit the vet when their pet is sick, but routine vet visits help detect problems early and prevent diseases before they become serious. Just like humans need regular doctor visits, cats also require consistent medical care to ensure they live long, happy lives. These visits are essential even if your cat looks perfectly healthy because some illnesses do not show obvious symptoms until they become severe.

Your cat's health needs change with age, so vet visits should be adjusted accordingly. Kittens, adult cats, and senior cats all have different requirements. A kitten may need frequent visits for vaccinations and early health assessments, while an adult cat generally requires an annual checkup. Older cats may need visits twice a year to monitor aging-related conditions such as arthritis, kidney disease, or dental problems. Whether your cat is young or old, regular checkups ensure that they stay in the best possible health.

A standard vet visit usually includes a physical examination where the veterinarian checks your cat's weight, body condition, coat health, eyes, ears, mouth, and teeth. They will also listen to the heart and lungs, feel the abdomen for any abnormalities, and assess the joints and muscles. The vet might also ask about your cat's eating habits, litter box behavior, and activity levels to identify any signs of health issues. If necessary, blood tests, urine analysis, or imaging such as X-rays may be recommended to check for underlying conditions.

Parasite prevention is another key part of routine checkups. Even indoor cats can get fleas, ticks, or intestinal worms, so your vet will discuss the best preventative treatments. If your cat is allowed outside or interacts with other animals, they might also need additional parasite control measures. Dental health is another concern, as many cats develop gum disease or tooth decay that can lead to infections and difficulty eating. Regular dental checkups and cleanings can prevent these problems from worsening.

Weight management is often addressed during vet visits, as obesity is a common problem in cats. An overweight cat is at a higher risk of developing diabetes, heart disease, and joint problems. Your vet will guide you on proper feeding, portion control, and the best type of food for your cat's specific needs. If your cat is underweight, the vet will investigate potential causes such as parasites, dental disease, or underlying medical conditions.

Behavioral assessments are also included in routine visits. If your cat has shown signs of aggression, excessive hiding, overgrooming, or sudden changes in behavior, a vet visit can help determine if there is a medical reason behind it. Sometimes, stress or environmental factors can affect a cat's behavior, and a vet can provide advice on how to improve their well-being.

Annual bloodwork is often recommended for adult cats to check for signs of kidney disease, liver problems, diabetes, and other hidden conditions. Senior cats, in particular, benefit from regular blood tests to catch age-related illnesses early. In some cases, a fecal examination may be done to check for parasites, especially if your cat has digestive issues.

If your cat is not already spayed or neutered, your vet will likely discuss the benefits of this procedure. Spaying and neutering not only prevent unwanted litters but also reduce the risk of certain cancers and behavioral issues. Additionally, your vet may recommend microchipping during a routine visit. This small chip, implanted under the skin, contains your contact information and can help reunite you with your cat if they ever get lost.

The frequency of vet visits depends on your cat's overall health. A healthy adult cat should visit the vet at least once a year, while kittens, senior cats, and cats with chronic conditions may need more frequent checkups. If your cat has an ongoing medical issue, your vet may suggest a customized schedule based on their needs.

Even if your cat dislikes the vet, it is crucial to make these visits as stress-free as possible. Start by using a comfortable carrier lined with a soft blanket and placing familiar scents inside. If your cat is especially anxious, covering the carrier with a towel and using calming sprays can help. Taking short car rides with your cat outside of vet visits may also reduce their stress over time.

Missing routine checkups can lead to undetected health problems, which might become serious before symptoms appear. Cats are experts at hiding pain and discomfort, so regular vet visits are essential for catching diseases in their early stages. Early detection often means simpler treatments, lower medical costs, and a better quality of life for your pet.

A common mistake cat owners make is assuming their pet is fine just because they seem active and eat well. Many conditions, such as kidney disease, heart problems, and dental infections, develop silently over time. By the time symptoms become noticeable, the disease may have already progressed significantly. Preventative care through regular vet visits can add years to your cat's life and prevent unnecessary suffering.

If you haven't taken your cat for a checkup in over a year, schedule an appointment as soon as possible. Keeping up with routine vet visits is one of the simplest and most effective ways to ensure your cat stays healthy and happy.

Vaccinations and Preventative Care

Keeping your cat healthy requires more than just food, shelter, and love. Vaccinations and preventative care play a crucial role in protecting your pet from serious illnesses. Cats, like humans, can be exposed to viruses, bacteria, and parasites that may lead to severe health complications. Vaccines help the immune system recognize and fight these threats before they become dangerous. Preventative care, including parasite control and regular checkups, ensures that small issues do not turn into major health problems.

Vaccinations are divided into core and non-core categories. Core vaccines are essential for all cats, regardless of their lifestyle. These include the rabies vaccine, feline panleukopenia (feline distemper), feline calicivirus, and feline herpesvirus. These diseases are highly contagious and often fatal, so vaccinating against them is a standard part of responsible cat care. Non-core vaccines are given based on a cat's risk factors. If your cat goes outdoors or interacts with other animals, they may need additional protection against diseases such as feline leukemia virus (FeLV) and feline immunodeficiency virus (FIV). Your veterinarian will determine the best vaccination schedule based on your cat's specific needs.

Kittens require a series of vaccinations to build their immune systems. The first vaccines are typically given at 6 to 8 weeks old, followed by booster shots every few weeks until they are about 16 weeks old. These initial vaccinations provide essential protection during the early stages of life when kittens are most vulnerable to infections. After the kitten series, booster shots are needed throughout adulthood, usually once a year or every three years, depending on the vaccine type. Rabies vaccinations are legally required in many places and must be kept up to date.

Beyond vaccinations, preventative care includes protecting your cat from parasites such as fleas, ticks, and worms. Even indoor cats can get parasites through contact with humans, other pets, or contaminated surfaces. Fleas cause itching, skin infections, and allergic reactions, while ticks can transmit diseases such as Lyme disease. Heartworms, though more commonly associated with dogs, can also affect cats and lead to severe respiratory problems. Monthly flea, tick, and heartworm preventatives are available in topical or oral forms and should be used consistently as recommended by your vet.

Internal parasites, such as roundworms, hookworms, and tapeworms, can affect a cat's digestive system, leading to weight loss, vomiting, and diarrhea. Regular deworming, especially for kittens, helps prevent these infections. A fecal examination at the vet can detect parasites, and appropriate medications will be prescribed if needed. Keeping litter boxes clean and practicing good hygiene reduces the risk of parasite transmission.

Dental care is another important part of preventative health. Many cats suffer from gum disease, which can lead to pain, infections, and even organ damage if bacteria spread through the bloodstream. Brushing your cat's teeth regularly, offering dental treats, and scheduling professional cleanings when necessary can help maintain oral health. Signs of dental problems include bad breath, difficulty eating, and excessive drooling.

A proper diet is a fundamental aspect of preventative care. Feeding your cat high-quality food that meets their nutritional needs helps prevent obesity, diabetes, and digestive issues. Cats are obligate carnivores, meaning they require animal protein for optimal health. A balanced diet, along with portion control, prevents excessive weight gain, which is a leading cause of many health problems in cats. If your cat gains or loses weight suddenly, a vet visit is necessary to rule out any underlying conditions.

Hydration is equally important. Cats have a low thirst drive, which makes them prone to dehydration and urinary tract issues. Providing fresh water at all times and incorporating wet food into their diet can help maintain proper hydration. If your cat refuses to drink water, investing in a cat water fountain may encourage better hydration.

Regular vet visits complement vaccinations and preventative care. During these visits, the vet will perform health checks, assess weight, examine the coat and skin, and discuss any behavioral changes. Blood tests, urine analysis, and fecal exams may be recommended to detect hidden health problems. Early detection of diseases through routine screenings makes treatment more effective and increases your cat's chances of a long, healthy life.

Some preventative measures are specific to a cat's lifestyle. Indoor cats generally have fewer health risks than outdoor cats, but they are still susceptible to respiratory infections, obesity, and stress-related conditions. Ensuring they have enough mental and physical stimulation through interactive play, scratching posts, and window perches helps maintain their well-being. Outdoor cats, on the other hand, face higher risks of injuries, infections, and exposure to parasites. They require extra protection through vaccinations, parasite prevention, and regular health checkups. If possible, keeping cats indoors or providing a secure outdoor enclosure reduces these risks.

Ignoring vaccinations and preventative care can have serious consequences. Many feline diseases are preventable, but once contracted, they can be difficult and expensive to treat. A single vet visit for a sick cat can cost significantly more than routine preventive measures. Failing to protect your cat from parasites may result in discomfort, illness, and even transmission to humans. Preventable conditions such as dental disease and obesity can lead to long-term suffering if not addressed early.

If you have not updated your cat's vaccinations or started a preventative care routine, now is the time to do so. Regular vet checkups, a healthy diet, parasite prevention, and proper dental care will keep your cat happy, comfortable, and protected from avoidable health risks. Taking these simple steps ensures a better quality of life for your feline companion.

Common Cat Health Issues

Cats are generally resilient animals, but they are not immune to health problems. Many conditions can affect their well-being, ranging from minor issues to serious illnesses. Understanding the most common health problems in cats allows you to recognize symptoms early and seek veterinary care before they become severe. Cats often hide their discomfort, making it even more important to stay vigilant about changes in their behavior, eating habits, and overall health. Preventative care, routine checkups, and a healthy lifestyle can help reduce the risk of many common ailments.

One of the most frequent health problems in cats is urinary tract disease, particularly Feline Lower Urinary Tract Disease (FLUTD). This condition affects the bladder and urethra, causing painful urination, frequent trips to the litter box, and sometimes blood in the urine. Stress, dehydration, obesity, and poor diet can contribute to FLUTD. Male cats are especially vulnerable because their narrower urethras can become blocked, leading to a life-threatening emergency. Providing fresh water, feeding a proper diet, and keeping stress levels low can help prevent urinary issues. If your cat strains to urinate or shows signs of distress near the litter box, immediate veterinary attention is required.

Dental disease is another common yet often overlooked problem. Many cats develop gingivitis, periodontal disease, or tooth decay due to plaque buildup. Bad breath, drooling, pawing at the mouth, and difficulty eating are signs of dental issues. If left untreated, oral infections can spread to other organs, leading to serious complications. Regular tooth brushing, dental treats, and professional cleanings help prevent these problems. A vet should examine any cat showing signs of mouth pain to determine if extractions or other treatments are necessary.

Obesity is a widespread health issue in domestic cats, particularly those who live indoors. Overweight cats are at higher risk for diabetes, arthritis, liver disease, and heart conditions. Excess weight puts stress on the joints, making movement difficult and leading to a sedentary lifestyle that further worsens the problem. Feeding measured portions of high-quality food, limiting treats, and encouraging daily exercise through play can help maintain a healthy weight. If a cat is already overweight, gradual weight loss under veterinary supervision is the safest approach. Sudden starvation can cause hepatic lipidosis, a potentially fatal liver condition.

Parasites, both internal and external, pose a major health risk to cats. Fleas are the most common external parasites, causing itching, allergies, and, in severe cases, anemia. Ticks can transmit serious infections, while ear mites lead to intense scratching and ear infections. Deworming is essential for eliminating intestinal parasites such as roundworms, tapeworms, and hookworms, which can affect digestion and overall health. Even cats that do not go outside can be exposed to parasites through human contact or contaminated surfaces. Monthly flea and tick preventatives, regular deworming, and keeping living areas clean help protect cats from infestations.

Respiratory infections, particularly those caused by feline herpesvirus and calicivirus, are highly contagious and can spread through direct contact or contaminated surfaces. Symptoms include sneezing, nasal discharge, coughing, and watery eyes. Kittens and older cats with weakened immune systems are especially vulnerable. Vaccination is the best prevention, but infected cats should also be kept in a warm, stress-free environment with easy access to food and water. Severe infections may require antibiotics or other medications prescribed by a veterinarian.

Kidney disease is a leading cause of illness in senior cats. The kidneys play a crucial role in filtering toxins from the blood, but as cats age, kidney function may decline. Symptoms include excessive thirst, frequent urination, weight loss, vomiting, and lethargy. While kidney disease cannot be cured, early detection allows for better management through diet changes, hydration therapy, and medications. Feeding high-quality, moisture-rich food and encouraging water intake can support kidney health and slow disease progression. Routine bloodwork in older cats helps catch kidney disease before symptoms appear.

Hyperthyroidism, a condition caused by an overactive thyroid gland, is another common issue in aging cats. It leads to increased metabolism, weight loss despite a good appetite, restlessness, and excessive thirst. Hyperthyroidism is usually treatable with medication, diet modifications, or, in some cases, radioactive iodine therapy. Left untreated, it can cause high blood pressure, heart disease, and organ damage. Any cat experiencing unexplained weight loss or hyperactivity should be evaluated by a vet to rule out thyroid problems.

Diabetes is a metabolic disorder that affects a cat's ability to regulate blood sugar. It often develops in overweight cats and causes increased thirst, frequent urination, weight loss, and lethargy. Treatment includes insulin injections, dietary adjustments, and close monitoring. With proper management, diabetic cats can live full, healthy lives. However, without treatment, diabetes can lead to severe complications and even death. Preventing obesity through proper diet and exercise reduces the risk of diabetes.

Cancer is another serious concern, with lymphoma being one of the most common types found in cats. Symptoms vary depending on the affected area but may include unexplained weight loss, vomiting, lethargy, and lumps under the skin. Early detection improves the chances of successful treatment, which may include surgery, chemotherapy, or supportive care. While not all cancers can be prevented, routine vet visits and monitoring for unusual changes in a cat's body or behavior increase the likelihood of early diagnosis.

Ignoring signs of illness in cats can lead to unnecessary suffering and complicated treatment plans. Cats instinctively hide pain, so by the time symptoms become noticeable, a disease may already be advanced. Regular vet checkups, a balanced diet, weight management, dental care, and parasite prevention all contribute to long-term health. If a cat shows any persistent changes in behavior, appetite, or energy levels, a vet visit should not be delayed. Catching problems early makes treatment easier, less expensive, and more effective in ensuring a better quality of life.

Parting Words on Chapter

Caring for a cat's health requires attention, consistency, and early intervention. Routine vet visits, proper nutrition, and preventative care minimize risks and ensure a happier life. Ignoring minor symptoms can lead to severe health issues, making observation and timely action essential for long-term well-being.

CHAPTER 6:
GROOMING YOUR CAT

Grooming is the process of maintaining a cat's cleanliness, coat health, and overall hygiene. It is essential for preventing common issues like matting, excessive shedding, and skin infections. Regular grooming also reduces hairballs and keeps nails, ears, and teeth in good condition. Cats groom themselves naturally, but human care is necessary to manage areas they cannot reach and to address specific needs based on breed, coat type, and lifestyle. Proper grooming promotes comfort, strengthens the bond between cat and owner, and contributes to long-term health. Understanding the right techniques ensures a stress-free experience while keeping a cat clean and healthy.

Bathing and Brushing

Cats are naturally clean animals, often seen grooming themselves for hours each day. Their tongues are like built-in brushes, designed to remove dirt and loose fur. However, despite their self-cleaning habits, they still need your help to maintain a clean and healthy coat. Bathing and brushing are essential parts of cat care, especially for long-haired breeds that are prone to matting. While short-haired cats may not need baths as often, regular brushing can prevent hairballs and reduce shedding. Understanding how and when to bathe your cat, as well as the right way to brush their fur, will ensure they stay comfortable, healthy, and happy.

Cats are not big fans of water, so bathing them can be a challenge. However, there are times when a bath becomes necessary. If your cat gets into something sticky, oily, or harmful, you may need to give them a proper wash. Some cats, especially those with skin conditions or allergies, may also require medicated baths prescribed by a vet. The key to a stress-free bath is preparation. Before you even introduce your cat to water, gather all the essentials. You'll need a cat-friendly shampoo (never use human shampoo as it can dry out their skin), a small container or a gentle spray nozzle, warm water, soft towels, and possibly a rubber mat to prevent slipping.

The best approach Is to introduce your cat to water gradually. Fill a sink or bathtub with just a few inches of lukewarm water. Cats are more comfortable when their feet touch the bottom, so avoid deep water. Speak to your cat in a calm, reassuring voice, and gently lower them into the water. Using a cup or a handheld sprayer, wet their fur slowly while avoiding their head and ears. Massage the shampoo into their coat using gentle motions, then rinse thoroughly. Leftover shampoo can irritate their skin, so make sure no residue remains. If needed, use a damp cloth to wipe their face instead of pouring water over their head.

Once the bath is done, wrap your cat in a soft towel and gently pat them dry. Some cats tolerate hairdryers on the lowest setting, but many are scared of the noise. If your cat doesn't like the dryer, let them air dry in a warm, draft-free room. Keep them indoors until they are completely dry to prevent chills. If you find that your cat becomes extremely stressed during baths, consider using waterless cat shampoos or pet wipes for occasional cleanups.

Brushing your cat's fur is just as important as bathing—if not more. Regular brushing removes dirt, reduces shedding, and prevents painful mats from forming. It also helps distribute natural oils across the coat, keeping it shiny and healthy. The type of brush you use depends on your cat's fur length. For short-haired cats, a rubber brush or a soft-bristled brush works best. Long-haired cats need more attention, and a combination of a wide-tooth comb and a slicker brush will help detangle their fur.

The best time to brush your cat is when they are relaxed. Try brushing after a meal or during a quiet moment when they're already lying down. Start with slow, gentle strokes, and let them get used to the sensation. Always brush in the direction of hair growth to avoid discomfort. If you encounter any tangles, do not pull on them—use your fingers or a detangling spray to gently loosen the knots. For long-haired breeds like Persians and Maine Coons, daily brushing is essential to prevent matting, which can be painful and even lead to skin infections.

Shedding is a natural process, but excessive loose fur can lead to hairballs. Brushing helps reduce the amount of fur your cat swallows while grooming themselves. If you notice that your cat is shedding more than usual, it could be due to seasonal changes, stress, or dietary issues. Adding omega-3 fatty acids to their diet or providing high-quality cat food can improve coat health and reduce shedding.

While brushing, take the opportunity to check your cat's skin for any abnormalities. Look for signs of fleas, redness, or dry patches. If you notice excessive scratching, hair loss, or sores, a visit to the vet may be necessary. Skin conditions can sometimes indicate allergies or underlying health issues that need attention.

Cats enjoy routine, so making brushing a regular habit will help them feel comfortable. If your cat resists brushing at first, start with short sessions and reward them with treats or praise. Over time, they will associate brushing with positive experiences. Some cats even enjoy the process, treating it as a form of petting and bonding time with you.

If you own a long-haired cat, professional grooming may be necessary from time to time, especially if their fur becomes severely matted. Mats can be painful and difficult to remove, sometimes requiring shaving by a professional groomer. To avoid this, make brushing a daily habit and keep an eye on areas prone to tangling, such as behind the ears and under the legs.

Avoid bathing your cat too frequently. Unlike dogs, cats do not need regular baths unless they are particularly dirty or have a medical condition that requires it. Overbathing can strip their skin of essential oils, leading to dryness and irritation. If you must bathe your cat, limit it to once every few months unless advised otherwise by a vet.

Always use cat-safe grooming products. Human shampoos and conditioners contain chemicals that can be harmful to cats, even if they seem mild to us. Stick to shampoos made specifically for cats, and avoid products with artificial fragrances or harsh ingredients.

Never force a bath on a terrified cat. If your cat becomes aggressive or panicked, stop and try a different approach, such as using grooming wipes or dry shampoo. A traumatic experience can make future grooming sessions even harder.

By making bathing and brushing a regular and positive experience, you will help your cat maintain a clean, healthy coat while strengthening your bond with them. Patience and consistency are key, and with time, your cat may even start to enjoy the process.

Nail Trimming and Ear Care

Caring for your cat goes beyond feeding and playtime. Their nails and ears need regular attention to prevent health issues and ensure their comfort. Overgrown nails can cause pain, affect their ability to walk, and lead to infections. Dirty ears, on the other hand, may result in wax buildup, mites, or bacterial infections. While many cats naturally wear down their nails through scratching, regular trimming is still necessary to prevent overgrowth and sharp claws. Ear care is just as important, especially for breeds prone to wax buildup or those with ear infections. Learning the proper techniques for nail trimming and ear cleaning will make the process easier for both you and your cat.

Trimming your cat's nails may seem like a daunting task, especially if your cat resists being handled. However, with patience and the right tools, it can be a stress-free routine. Cats have retractable claws, which means you need to gently press on their paws to extend the nails. The goal is to trim just the sharp tip without cutting too close to the pinkish area inside the nail, called the quick. The quick contains nerves and blood vessels, and cutting it can cause pain and bleeding. If you're new to nail trimming, start by clipping just a small portion of the tip to avoid accidents.

Using the right tools makes a big difference. Cat-specific nail clippers or human nail clippers with a straight edge work well. Guillotine-style clippers are another option, but they require more control. Always ensure the clippers are sharp to avoid crushing the nail. Dull blades can cause splitting or uneven cuts, making the process more uncomfortable for your cat.

The best time to trim nails is when your cat is calm. After a meal or during a relaxed moment, gently hold your cat's paw and press the pad to extend the nails. If your cat is not used to having their paws handled, start with short sessions where you simply touch and massage their paws without trimming. Reward them with treats or praise to build positive associations. When they are comfortable, trim one or two nails at a time until they get used to the process. If your cat becomes stressed, take a break and try again later.

If you accidentally cut the quick and bleeding occurs, remain calm. Use styptic powder, cornstarch, or a clean cloth to stop the bleeding. Applying gentle pressure for a few seconds usually helps. While a small cut heals quickly, it's best to be careful and trim little by little. If your cat refuses nail trimming entirely, consider getting help from a professional groomer or veterinarian.

Scratching posts are essential for maintaining healthy nails. They allow cats to shed the outer layers of their claws naturally, keeping them in good condition. Providing different textures, such as sisal, cardboard, or wood, can encourage your cat to use scratching posts instead of furniture. Regular scratching helps reduce the need for frequent nail trims, though trimming is still necessary every few weeks.

Ear care is another essential aspect of grooming. Unlike dogs, cats do not need frequent ear cleaning, but checking their ears regularly can help prevent infections. A healthy cat's ears should be pink, clean, and free of any strong odor. Wax buildup, excessive dirt, or a foul smell may indicate an issue. If your cat frequently shakes their head, scratches their ears, or tilts their head, it could be a sign of ear mites, infection, or an allergy.

Cleaning your cat's ears should be done with caution. Use a vet-approved ear cleaner and cotton pads or gauze. Avoid using cotton swabs (Q-tips), as they can push debris further into the ear canal and cause damage. To clean, gently hold your cat's head and lift one ear flap. Apply a few drops of the ear cleaner, then massage the base of the ear to help loosen wax and debris. Let your cat shake their head to remove excess liquid. Use a clean cotton pad to wipe away any remaining dirt. Repeat the process on the other ear if necessary.

If you notice black, crumbly debris in your cat's ears, it may indicate ear mites. These tiny parasites cause irritation and can lead to secondary infections if untreated. A visit to the vet is necessary for proper diagnosis and treatment. Ear infections can also be caused by bacteria, yeast, or allergies. If your cat's ears are red, inflamed, or have a strong smell, consult a veterinarian for appropriate treatment.

Some breeds, particularly those with folded ears like Scottish Folds, require extra attention. Their ear structure can trap dirt and moisture, making them more prone to infections. Regular checks and gentle cleaning can prevent issues from developing.

Routine nail trimming and ear care not only keep your cat healthy but also strengthen your bond. Handling their paws and ears from a young age helps them become more comfortable with grooming. If your cat resists or becomes agitated, take things slowly and use treats to create a positive experience.

Never attempt to trim nails or clean ears forcefully. If your cat becomes too stressed, stop and try again later. For severely overgrown nails or persistent ear problems, seek professional help. Using improper techniques or the wrong tools can cause injury or discomfort. Always choose vet-recommended grooming products and handle your cat gently to make the experience as stress-free as possible.

Dental Health and Hygiene

Your cat's dental health is just as important as their diet, grooming, and exercise. Many cat owners overlook oral care, assuming that cats naturally maintain their teeth, but this is not true. Without proper dental hygiene, plaque and tartar build up, leading to gum disease, infections, and even tooth loss. Poor oral health can also contribute to serious health conditions, as bacteria from the mouth can enter the bloodstream and affect vital organs like the heart and kidneys. Regular dental care ensures your cat remains healthy, pain-free, and able to eat comfortably. Understanding the best practices for brushing, diet, and professional dental check-ups will help you maintain your cat's oral health effectively.

Brushing your cat's teeth is the most effective way to prevent dental issues. While it may seem challenging at first, introducing it gradually can make it a routine part of your cat's care. Start by getting your cat comfortable with having their mouth touched. Gently lift their lips and rub their gums with your finger for a few seconds each day. Once they tolerate this, introduce a cat-specific toothpaste. Never use human toothpaste, as it contains ingredients like fluoride and xylitol, which are toxic to cats. Cat toothpaste is specially formulated with safe ingredients and often comes in flavors like chicken or seafood to make the experience more appealing.

Choosing the right toothbrush is equally important. A small, soft-bristled cat toothbrush or a finger brush works best. If your cat resists brushing, start by applying a small amount of toothpaste to their lips or gums so they get used to the taste. Gradually introduce the toothbrush by letting them sniff it and feel it against their teeth. Once they are comfortable, gently brush their teeth using slow, circular motions. Focus on the outer surfaces, as this is where plaque accumulates the most. You don't need to brush the inner sides, as a cat's tongue naturally helps keep those areas clean.

Brushing at least three times a week is recommended, but daily brushing is ideal for preventing plaque buildup. If your cat strongly resists brushing, consider alternatives like dental wipes or oral gels. These products help reduce bacteria and freshen breath, though they are not as effective as brushing.

Diet also plays a significant role in your cat's dental health. Dry kibble is often believed to help clean teeth, but not all cat food provides dental benefits. Some specially formulated dental diets contain larger kibble pieces that require more chewing, helping to scrape off plaque. Look for vet-approved dental diets or treats that contain ingredients designed to break down tartar and promote oral health.

Raw bones, such as chicken necks, can also help with dental hygiene by providing natural chewing resistance. However, bones should always be raw, as cooked bones can splinter and cause serious internal injuries. Always consult your veterinarian before introducing bones into your cat's diet.

Water additives are another option for improving oral hygiene. These are liquid solutions added to your cat's drinking water, helping to reduce bacteria and plaque formation. While not a replacement for brushing, they can be a helpful supplement, especially for cats that resist other forms of dental care.

Professional dental cleanings may be necessary if your cat develops severe tartar buildup or gum disease. Vets perform these cleanings under anesthesia to remove hardened plaque and check for underlying dental problems. Signs that your cat may need a professional cleaning include bad breath, difficulty eating, excessive drooling, bleeding gums, or visible yellow or brown tartar on the teeth. If left untreated, dental disease can lead to painful infections and even tooth extractions. Regular veterinary check-ups allow early detection of dental issues before they become serious.

Some cats, particularly certain breeds like Persians and Siamese, are more prone to dental problems due to their jaw structure or genetics. Regular dental care is even more critical for these breeds to prevent early tooth loss or chronic gum issues.

Dental health is closely linked to overall well-being, so neglecting it can lead to bigger health problems. Bacteria from untreated gum infections can enter the bloodstream, potentially affecting the kidneys, liver, and heart. This is why regular dental care is not just about fresh breath—it is about protecting your cat's long-term health.

Never attempt to use human dental products on your cat. Ingredients like mint, fluoride, and alcohol are harmful to felines, even in small amounts. If your cat shows signs of severe dental pain, such as refusing to eat or pawing at their mouth, seek veterinary attention immediately. Starting dental care early and maintaining consistency will help your cat stay comfortable and healthy, ensuring they enjoy a pain-free life.

Parting Words on Chapter

Consistent grooming prevents health issues and strengthens the connection between cat and owner. Keeping a calm approach, using the right tools, and introducing grooming gradually make the process easier. A well-groomed cat is happier, healthier, and more comfortable in its daily life.

CHAPTER 7: CAT BEHAVIOR AND TRAINING

Cat behavior refers to the actions, instincts, and responses that shape how a cat interacts with its environment, people, and other animals. Understanding these behaviors is essential for creating a comfortable home and fostering a positive relationship. Training builds on this knowledge, helping guide natural instincts toward acceptable habits. A well-trained cat is easier to manage, less likely to develop destructive behaviors, and more responsive to communication. Addressing issues like litter box habits, command learning, and aggression improves daily life for both the cat and its owner. Establishing clear expectations and reinforcing positive actions ensures a stress-free and cooperative pet.

Litter Box Training

Cats are naturally clean animals, and most of them take to using a litter box quite easily. However, if you're introducing a kitten or even an older cat to a new home, litter box training is an essential step. Proper training ensures that your cat knows where to relieve itself, keeping your home clean and odor-free. The good news is that cats instinctively prefer to bury their waste, so with the right guidance, patience, and setup, your feline friend will quickly learn to use the litter box consistently.

Litter box training starts with choosing the right box. Cats come in different sizes, and their litter boxes should match their needs. Kittens and small cats require a box with low sides so they can easily step in and out. For larger cats, a bigger box ensures comfort. Covered litter boxes provide privacy, but some cats dislike them due to the trapped odors. Open litter boxes, on the other hand, offer easy access and better ventilation. The key is to observe your cat's preference. If you notice resistance, switching to a different style might make the transition easier.

Placement of the litter box is just as important as the box itself. You need to put it in a quiet, low-traffic area where your cat can have some privacy. Cats dislike noisy or busy spaces, so placing the box near a washing machine, in a hallway, or too close to their food and water can discourage use. If you have multiple floors in your home, having a litter box on each level will help prevent accidents. For households with multiple cats, the general rule is to provide one litter box per cat, plus an extra one. This helps to prevent territorial issues and ensures that no cat feels forced to use an unclean box.

Choosing the right litter is another key factor. Cats can be particular about texture and scent. Some prefer fine-grain litter because it's softer on their paws, while others may like larger granules. Clumping litter makes it easier for you to scoop out waste and control odors, while non-clumping litter requires more frequent changing but is often dust-free. Scented litter might appeal to humans, but many cats dislike strong fragrances, so unscented options are usually the safest choice. If your cat refuses to use the litter box, the type of litter might be the issue. Gradually transitioning to a different kind by mixing it with the old litter can help your cat adjust without stress.

Once the setup is complete, introduce your cat to the litter box. If you have a kitten, gently place it inside the box after meals and naps. Scratch the litter with your fingers to show how it works. Most kittens instinctively begin digging and using the box without much encouragement. For older cats, especially those used to outdoor environments, placing a small amount of their previous waste in the box can signal that this is the appropriate place to go. If your cat shows hesitation, patience is key. Never force your cat into the box, as it can create a negative association.

Cleaning the litter box regularly is essential for keeping your cat's habits consistent. Cats dislike dirty litter boxes and may start avoiding them if they aren't cleaned frequently. Scooping out waste at least once a day prevents odors from building up and keeps the litter fresh. A full litter change should be done weekly, along with washing the box with mild soap and warm water. Avoid strong chemicals, as they can leave a scent that repels cats. If you notice your cat suddenly avoiding the litter box, an unclean environment could be the reason.

Sometimes, even with the right setup, accidents happen. If your cat eliminates outside the box, avoid punishing it. Instead, clean the area thoroughly with an enzyme-based cleaner to remove the scent, preventing repeat accidents. If your cat consistently refuses to use the box, a medical issue such as a urinary tract infection or digestive problem could be the cause. Consulting a veterinarian ensures that health concerns are ruled out before assuming it's a behavioral issue.

Training takes time, and every cat learns at its own pace. Some will pick it up within a day, while others may take weeks. If your cat initially struggles, patience and consistency will make a difference. Praise and gentle encouragement help reinforce good behavior. If needed, confining a new cat to a small space with the litter box for a few days can help it learn more quickly. Once it starts using the box consistently, you can gradually give it access to more areas of the house.

A well-trained cat makes life easier for both of you. By choosing the right litter box, placing it in a suitable location, and maintaining cleanliness, you create an environment where your cat feels comfortable and confident. If issues arise, they can often be resolved by adjusting the setup or checking for underlying health problems. Ensuring that your cat has a stress-free and positive experience with the litter box is the key to long-term success.

Teaching Basic Commands

Training a cat may seem challenging, especially if you're used to the idea that only dogs respond to commands. However, cats are highly intelligent and can learn basic commands with patience, consistency, and the right motivation. Teaching your cat commands is not only a fun way to bond but also a useful way to ensure good behavior and safety. Whether you want your cat to come when called, sit, or even high-five, positive reinforcement and understanding your cat's natural instincts are the keys to success.

The first step in teaching basic commands is to find what motivates your cat. Unlike dogs, which are often eager to please, cats need a reason to participate. Food treats, such as small pieces of cooked chicken or store-bought cat treats, are excellent motivators. Some cats respond well to praise or petting, while others prefer interactive toys. Identifying what excites your cat will make training sessions more effective.

Start with the most useful and simple command: "Come." Teaching your cat to come when called is particularly helpful in situations where you need to get their attention quickly. Begin by choosing a consistent cue, such as saying your cat's name followed by the word "come." Stand a few feet away and call your cat while holding a treat. If the cat takes even a small step toward you, reward it immediately. Repeat this several times, gradually increasing the distance. Over time, your cat will associate the word with a positive reward and will start coming when called, even without a treat. This command works best when reinforced daily, especially before mealtime, since a hungry cat is more likely to respond.

Another useful command is "Sit." Teaching a cat to sit is a great way to keep them calm and prevent unwanted behavior, such as jumping onto tables during mealtime. Hold a treat close to your cat's nose, then slowly move it upward and slightly back. Your cat's natural reaction will be to sit as it follows the treat with its eyes. The moment your cat sits, say "Sit" and give the treat. Repeat this process several times, ensuring that your cat makes the connection between the word and the action. With enough repetition, your cat will sit on command even when there's no treat in sight.

"Stay" is another command that can be useful, especially when preventing your cat from darting out of a door or jumping onto forbidden surfaces. Start by having your cat sit, then hold up your hand like a stop sign and say "Stay" in a firm but gentle voice. Wait just a second or two before giving a treat. Gradually increase the waiting time before rewarding your cat. Since cats have shorter attention spans than dogs, keeping training sessions brief and rewarding success quickly is essential.

For playful cats, teaching a fun trick like "High-Five" can be an enjoyable challenge. Begin by holding a treat in your hand and letting your cat sniff it. Then, gently tap one of your cat's front paws while saying "High-Five." Some cats will instinctively raise their paw in response. When this happens, immediately give the treat. If your cat doesn't lift its paw on its own, you can try gently lifting it for them before giving the reward. With repetition, your cat will start lifting its paw on command, turning training into a fun game.

Training sessions should always be short and positive. Cats have a limited attention span, so working in five-minute intervals a few times a day is more effective than long sessions. Ending on a good note, even if progress is slow, helps your cat remain interested in learning. Never force your cat to participate, as this can create frustration and make training counterproductive. If your cat seems uninterested, try again later or switch to a different reward system.

Some cats learn faster than others, and personality plays a big role in training success. Curious and food-driven cats tend to pick up commands more quickly, while more independent or easily distracted cats may take longer. The key is consistency and patience. If your cat is struggling with a command, breaking it down into smaller steps can help. For example, if your cat won't sit, reward it for just lowering its body slightly at first, then build up to a full sitting position over multiple sessions.

Training not only strengthens the bond between you and your cat but also improves communication. A trained cat is more likely to listen to you in important situations, making everyday life easier. Commands like "Come" can be life-saving if your cat ever escapes outside, while "Stay" can prevent accidents indoors. Teaching basic commands also provides mental stimulation, reducing boredom and destructive behavior.

If training isn't going as planned, avoid using punishment. Yelling or scolding will only make your cat fearful and resistant to learning. Instead, focus on rewarding good behavior and ignoring mistakes. If your cat consistently ignores a command, reassess the training method, the reward being used, or the environment. Sometimes, distractions in the surroundings can make it harder for your cat to focus.

With patience and the right approach, any cat can learn basic commands. It may take time, but the rewards—both practical and emotional—are well worth the effort. Keep training sessions positive, be consistent with cues, and most importantly, make it a fun experience for your cat.

Managing Aggressive or Problem Behavior

Cats are often seen as independent and gentle creatures, but they can sometimes exhibit aggressive or problematic behavior. This can range from biting and scratching to excessive meowing or destructive tendencies. While aggression and misbehavior may seem random, they usually have underlying causes. Understanding why your cat acts out is the first step in correcting the behavior. Whether the aggression is directed at people, other animals, or even objects in the home, consistent training, patience, and the right techniques can help manage and reduce unwanted behavior.

Aggression in cats can take different forms. Play aggression is common in kittens and young cats, often showing up as biting and scratching during play. Since kittens learn social behavior from their littermates, those separated from their siblings too early may not understand how to control their bites. If your cat tends to bite or scratch too hard during play, immediately stopping the interaction can teach it that rough play means no play at all. Redirecting this energy to toys, such as feather wands or soft balls, can prevent your hands from becoming the target.

Fear-based aggression occurs when a cat feels threatened. If your cat hisses, growls, or swipes when approached, it may be reacting out of fear rather than hostility. New environments, unfamiliar people, loud noises, or past trauma can all contribute to fearful behavior. Giving your cat space and allowing it to approach on its own terms helps build trust. Avoid forcing interaction, and instead, use positive reinforcement, such as treats or soothing tones, to create a sense of safety.

Some cats show territorial aggression, particularly when another pet is introduced into the home. A cat that sees a newcomer as a threat may hiss, swat, or chase them away. This behavior is more common in cats that have been the sole pet for a long time. A slow introduction process can ease the tension. Keeping the new pet in a separate room at first and gradually allowing brief supervised interactions can help both animals adjust. Using scent-swapping techniques—such as exchanging bedding between the pets—can also reduce hostility by familiarizing them with each other's scent before physical introductions.

Redirected aggression happens when a cat becomes agitated by something it cannot directly attack and then lashes out at the nearest person or animal. For example, if your cat sees another cat outside through the window and cannot reach it, it may suddenly turn and bite you instead. If you notice your cat getting tense or fixating on something outside, distracting it with a toy or moving it to a different area can prevent an aggressive outburst. Avoid touching a highly agitated cat, as it may attack out of frustration.

Overstimulation can also trigger aggression, especially during petting. Some cats enjoy being stroked but have a limit before they become irritated. If your cat suddenly bites or swats while being petted, watch for warning signs such as tail flicking, ear flattening, or skin twitching. Learning your cat's body language can prevent overstimulation. If your cat prefers short petting sessions, respect its boundaries and stop before it becomes uncomfortable.

Destructive behavior, such as scratching furniture or knocking objects off shelves, is another common issue. Cats have a natural instinct to scratch to mark their territory and keep their claws healthy. Providing a variety of scratching posts and pads can prevent them from damaging furniture. Placing a scratching post near their favorite spot or using catnip to attract them to it encourages proper use. If your cat insists on scratching furniture, using deterrents such as double-sided tape or aluminum foil on the affected area can discourage the behavior.

Excessive meowing can be another frustrating problem. Some cats are naturally more vocal than others, but if your cat meows constantly, there may be an underlying reason. Hunger, attention-seeking, or stress can all cause excessive vocalization. Feeding your cat on a consistent schedule and providing enough play and mental stimulation can reduce unnecessary meowing. If your cat cries at night, ensuring it has food, water, and a comfortable sleeping space can help. However, if meowing suddenly increases without explanation, a vet check is recommended to rule out medical issues.

Litter box avoidance is a serious behavioral issue that requires immediate attention. If a cat starts urinating or defecating outside the litter box, the first step is to check for medical problems, such as urinary tract infections or kidney disease. If health concerns are ruled out, environmental factors may be to blame. A dirty litter box, the wrong type of litter, or a stressful home environment can all contribute to the problem. Keeping the litter box clean, experimenting with different types of litter, and reducing household stressors can help resolve the issue.

Managing aggressive or problem behavior takes time and patience. Punishment, such as yelling or hitting, will only make the behavior worse and damage your relationship with your cat. Instead, understanding the root cause and addressing it through positive reinforcement, redirection, and environmental changes will create a more harmonious living space for both you and your pet. If aggressive behavior persists despite all efforts, consulting a veterinarian or an animal behaviorist can provide additional guidance and solutions tailored to your cat's specific needs.

Parting Words on Chapter

Training and understanding a cat requires patience, consistency, and awareness of its natural instincts. Every cat learns at its own pace, and small adjustments can make a big difference. Reinforcing good behavior while preventing negative habits early creates a well-adjusted and cooperative feline companion.

Chapter 8: Socializing Your Cat

Socializing a cat means helping it feel comfortable around people, other animals, and new environments. A well-socialized cat is more confident, relaxed, and less likely to develop behavioral issues. Cats that feel secure in their surroundings form stronger bonds with their owners and adapt more easily to changes. Early and consistent socialization reduces stress, prevents aggression, and improves overall well-being. Understanding feline social behavior, introducing new experiences gradually, and respecting boundaries create a positive foundation for interaction. Each cat has a unique personality, but with patience and the right approach, even the most reserved cat can become more trusting.

Introducing a New Cat to Your Home

Bringing a new cat into your home is an exciting experience, but it also requires patience and preparation. Cats are territorial creatures, and a sudden change in environment can be stressful for them. Whether you're adopting a kitten or an adult cat, understanding how to make their transition smooth will help them settle in comfortably. A well-planned introduction minimizes anxiety, prevents behavioral issues, and strengthens the bond between you and your new feline companion.

Before bringing your cat home, prepare a designated space where they can feel safe. This area should be quiet, away from heavy foot traffic, and stocked with all the essentials—food, water, a litter box, a scratching post, and a comfortable resting place. Cats rely heavily on scent to understand their surroundings, so allowing them to become familiar with a small space before exploring the entire house helps reduce their stress. The goal is to create a secure environment where they can gradually adjust at their own pace.

Once you bring the cat home, avoid overwhelming them with too much attention. Instead, open their carrier inside the prepared space and allow them to come out on their own. Some cats might explore immediately, while others may prefer to hide for several hours or even days. This is normal, and forcing interaction can make them more anxious. Sit nearby and speak in a calm, reassuring voice, but let them initiate contact when they feel comfortable.

If you already have other pets, keep them separated initially. Cats communicate heavily through scent, so exchanging bedding or rubbing a cloth on each pet and placing it near the other helps them get accustomed to each other's presence. Supervised introductions should only happen once your new cat is comfortable in their environment and showing signs of confidence, such as eating regularly and exploring freely. During the first face-to-face meeting, keep interactions short and positive, using treats and praise to reinforce good behavior.

Food and litter box placement play a critical role in your cat's adjustment. Keep their litter box in a quiet, easily accessible location, separate from their food and water. If your home is large, consider placing multiple litter boxes to avoid accidents. Stick to a consistent feeding schedule, and if possible, use the same type of food the cat was eating before adoption. Sudden changes in diet can cause digestive issues, so any transitions should be gradual over several days.

Understanding feline body language helps you gauge how well your cat is adapting. Signs of relaxation include a slow-blinking gaze, soft body posture, and purring. If they tuck their tail, flatten their ears, or hide excessively, they might be feeling overwhelmed. Give them more time to adjust, and avoid making loud noises or sudden movements around them. Patience is key, and every cat adapts at their own pace.

Playtime and enrichment activities help your new cat feel more at home. Providing interactive toys, scratching posts, and window perches keeps them engaged and reduces anxiety. If your cat is hesitant to interact, using a wand toy or tossing treats gently can encourage them to engage without pressure. Creating positive associations with their new home builds their confidence and strengthens their trust in you.

Cats thrive on routine, so maintaining consistency in feeding times, play sessions, and social interactions is crucial. Avoid rearranging their environment too soon, as familiar smells and objects provide comfort. Over time, as they gain confidence, you can gradually introduce them to other parts of your home.

It's important to schedule a vet visit within the first week of adoption. This helps ensure your new cat is healthy, up-to-date on vaccinations, and free from parasites. A veterinarian can also provide guidance on diet, behavior, and any special care your cat may need. If your cat was recently spayed or neutered, monitoring their recovery and keeping them comfortable is essential.

Patience and understanding are vital in the first few weeks. Some cats may take only a few days to adjust, while others need weeks or even months. Rushing the process can lead to stress-related issues like hiding, aggression, or refusal to eat. Creating a positive, stress-free introduction makes a significant difference in how well your cat adapts to their new home.

Bringing a cat home is a long-term commitment, and the way you handle their first days sets the foundation for your future relationship. If you allow them to adjust at their own pace, provide a safe environment, and respect their boundaries, they will soon feel secure and happy in their new home.

Understanding Cat Social Dynamics

Cats are often misunderstood as solitary creatures, but they have a complex social structure that influences how they interact with humans, other cats, and even other pets. Understanding cat social dynamics is essential for creating a peaceful home environment, especially if you have multiple cats or plan to introduce a new one. Unlike dogs, who operate in hierarchical packs, cats establish loose territories and relationships based on comfort, trust, and familiarity rather than dominance.

In multi-cat households, each cat naturally forms a territory, which may be a specific area of the house, a favorite chair, or even a designated sleeping spot. Conflicts often arise when one cat encroaches on another's territory without invitation. This is why sudden introductions between unfamiliar cats can lead to hissing, swatting, or even fights. The key to maintaining harmony is to recognize each cat's need for personal space while also providing opportunities for positive interaction.

Cats use scent to communicate and establish their social structure. They have scent glands on their cheeks, paws, and base of the tail, which they use to mark their environment and other cats. When two cats rub against each other, they exchange scents, signaling trust and companionship. A bonded pair of cats will often groom each other, sleep close together, and share food bowls without issue. If your cats do not exhibit these behaviors, it does not necessarily mean they dislike each other—they may simply prefer maintaining their own space.

Aggression and tension between cats can be managed through careful observation and environmental adjustments. If one cat frequently chases, blocks access to food, or swats at another, it may indicate territorial disputes or competition for resources. To prevent conflict, ensure each cat has its own food and water bowls, litter boxes, and resting areas. Vertical spaces, such as cat trees or wall-mounted shelves, allow cats to establish their hierarchy naturally without resorting to physical fights.

Introducing a new cat into an established cat's territory requires patience. A gradual introduction process, involving scent swapping and short, supervised meetings, allows both cats to adjust to each other's presence without feeling threatened. Sudden, forced interactions can lead to long-term hostility. Even after a successful introduction, cats may take weeks or even months to fully accept each other.

Social dynamics also influence how cats interact with humans. Some cats are naturally social and seek constant attention, while others are more independent and prefer minimal interaction. Understanding a cat's body language is crucial in determining their comfort level. A cat that purrs, slow-blinks, or rubs against you is expressing affection, whereas a flicking tail, flattened ears, or dilated pupils indicate stress or agitation. Ignoring these signals can lead to unwanted behaviors such as biting or scratching.

Changes in household dynamics, such as moving to a new home, introducing a new pet, or altering feeding schedules, can disrupt a cat's sense of security. Stress in cats often manifests as hiding, excessive grooming, or litter box avoidance. To ease their anxiety, maintaining a consistent routine and providing familiar scents, such as unwashed bedding or pheromone diffusers, can help them feel more secure.

Understanding the unique personalities of your cats is just as important as recognizing their social structures. Some cats prefer companionship and thrive in multi-cat households, while others prefer solitude. Forcing social interaction on a cat that prefers independence can lead to stress and behavioral problems. Respecting their individual preferences allows them to coexist peacefully.

A well-balanced social environment benefits both cats and their owners. When cats feel secure in their territory and social structure, they exhibit fewer behavioral issues and form stronger bonds with their human caregivers. Encouraging positive interactions through playtime, treats, and affection helps reinforce trust and reduces conflict. Observing their interactions and adjusting the environment as needed ensures a happy and stress-free home for all.

Misinterpreting a cat's behavior or forcing social interactions can lead to tension and long-term behavioral issues. Always observe how your cats interact and respect their boundaries. If conflicts arise, never punish them physically—this only increases stress and damages trust. Instead, provide separate spaces and allow them to adjust naturally. With patience and understanding, you can create a home where each cat feels safe and respected.

Interacting with Your Cat and Building Trust

Cats are independent creatures, but that does not mean they do not crave companionship and affection. Unlike dogs, who often seek attention openly, cats form bonds in a more subtle and gradual way. Building trust with a cat requires patience, consistency, and an understanding of their unique way of communicating. Whether you have adopted a new cat or want to strengthen your relationship with an existing one, learning how to interact with them properly ensures a stronger and more fulfilling bond.

Establishing trust begins with respecting a cat's personal space. Cats are naturally cautious and may take time to feel comfortable around new people or environments. Approaching too quickly, forcing interaction, or trying to pick them up when they are not ready can make them wary of you. Instead, allow your cat to come to you on their own terms. Sitting quietly near them, offering a treat, or engaging in slow blinking—where you close your eyes gently and reopen them—can communicate that you are non-threatening. Cats often respond to this by blinking back, a sign of trust and relaxation.

Understanding body language is key to positive interactions. A relaxed cat will have their ears facing forward, their tail in a neutral position, and may knead their paws as a sign of comfort. Purring, gentle headbutting, and rubbing against you are ways they express affection. On the other hand, flattened ears, a flicking tail, and dilated pupils indicate stress or agitation. If your cat displays these signs, it is best to give them space rather than forcing interaction.

Handling a cat properly can also influence their trust in you. When picking up a cat, support their back legs and hold them close to your body to help them feel secure. Avoid lifting them suddenly or holding them in an uncomfortable position, as this can make them associate being picked up with discomfort. If your cat dislikes being held, respect their preference and interact with them in ways they enjoy, such as petting or playing.

Petting preferences vary among cats. Some enjoy being stroked along the back and under the chin, while others may prefer gentle scratches behind the ears. The base of the tail is a sensitive area that some cats love being petted, while others may react with irritation. Observing their reactions will help you understand what they enjoy. Always let them initiate petting sessions—if they lean into your hand or purr, it is a good sign they are comfortable. If they swish their tail or try to move away, stop and let them be.

Playtime is an essential part of building trust and strengthening your bond. Interactive toys such as wand toys, laser pointers, and feather teasers mimic a cat's natural hunting instincts and provide both physical and mental stimulation. Playing with your cat daily not only keeps them active and engaged but also helps them associate you with positive experiences.

Rotate toys regularly to keep them interested, and always allow them to "catch" the toy occasionally to satisfy their hunting instincts.

Consistency in routine builds security and trust. Cats thrive on predictability, so feeding them at the same times each day, maintaining a regular play schedule, and keeping their environment stable helps them feel secure. Sudden changes in their routine, such as shifting their feeding time or frequently moving their litter box, can cause stress and anxiety. If changes are necessary, introduce them gradually to prevent distress.

Treats can be an effective way to build trust and reinforce positive interactions. Offering treats when your cat approaches you, allows you to pet them, or engages in play helps create positive associations. However, treats should be given in moderation to avoid weight issues. High-quality treats or small pieces of cooked meat can be used to reward good behavior, such as using the scratching post instead of furniture.

Some cats take longer to trust than others, especially if they have had negative experiences with humans in the past. Rescue cats, in particular, may be more hesitant and require extra patience. Speaking in a calm voice, moving slowly, and respecting their boundaries go a long way in helping them feel safe. For particularly shy cats, sitting in the same room without attempting interaction can help them grow accustomed to your presence. Over time, they will begin to associate you with security rather than fear.

Overstimulation is something to be mindful of when interacting with a cat. While petting and playing are important, some cats have a limit to how much they can tolerate at once. A cat that suddenly bites or swats after a period of petting may be experiencing overstimulation. This is not aggression but rather a signal that they need a break. Learning to recognize early warning signs, such as tail twitching or skin rippling, can help prevent negative interactions.

Earning a cat's trust is a gradual process that requires patience and attentiveness. Rushing the bond or forcing interaction can have the opposite effect, making them more withdrawn or defensive. If a cat exhibits fearful or aggressive behavior, never punish them physically, as this will damage trust and make them associate you with fear. Instead, focus on creating a safe and comfortable environment where they can feel at ease. With time and consistency, even the most reserved cat can develop a deep and trusting bond with their caregiver.

Parting Words on Chapter

Understanding and respecting a cat's social nature creates a harmonious home and a stronger bond. Rushing socialization or ignoring boundaries leads to stress and behavioral issues. Patience, positive reinforcement, and consistency help build trust, making interactions enjoyable for both the cat and owner.

CHAPTER 9: RECOGNIZING SIGNS OF STRESS AND ILLNESS

Recognizing signs of stress and illness in cats is essential for ensuring their well-being. Cats instinctively hide pain and discomfort, making it difficult to detect health issues early. Behavioral changes, appetite fluctuations, and unusual grooming habits often indicate underlying problems that require attention. Early intervention prevents minor issues from developing into severe conditions, improving a cat's quality of life. Understanding these signals helps in providing timely medical care, maintaining emotional stability, and creating a comfortable environment. Awareness of both physical and behavioral symptoms allows for prompt action, reducing risks and ensuring a healthier, happier life for feline companions.

Common Signs of Stress in Cats

Cats are naturally independent and resilient animals, but they can experience stress just like humans. Unlike dogs, who may openly express their emotions, cats tend to hide their discomfort, making it challenging for you to recognize when they are stressed. Stress in cats can be triggered by changes in their environment, health issues, or disruptions to their routine. If left unchecked, stress can lead to behavioral problems, a weakened immune system, and even serious health conditions. Understanding the common signs of stress in your cat is essential for maintaining their well-being and ensuring a happy, healthy life.

Your cat may not be able to tell you how they feel, but their body language, habits, and behaviors can give you important clues. The earlier you detect stress, the easier it is to manage and prevent further issues. Some signs are subtle, while others may be more obvious, but all of them require your attention.

One of the first signs of stress in cats is a change in their normal behavior. A typically affectionate cat may suddenly become withdrawn and hide more often, avoiding interaction with you or other pets. Conversely, a usually independent cat might become clingy, following you around the house and seeking constant reassurance. Changes in their usual personality should not be ignored, as they can indicate underlying anxiety.

Changes in eating and drinking habits are another major indicator of stress. If your cat suddenly stops eating or starts eating much less, it could be a sign that something is bothering them. On the other hand, some cats may overeat when stressed. An increase or decrease in water intake can also signal distress. If you notice changes in their appetite or hydration, monitor them closely and try to identify potential stressors.

Litter box issues are a common sign of stress. A cat that starts urinating or defecating outside their litter box is often trying to communicate that something is wrong. Stress can cause them to develop urinary tract infections or digestive problems, making it uncomfortable for them to use the litter box. Sometimes, they may avoid the litter box due to a negative association, such as a frightening noise nearby or an unclean environment. If your cat starts having accidents around the house, consider what might have changed in their surroundings.

Aggressive or destructive behavior is another sign to watch for. A stressed cat may become more irritable, hissing, growling, or even swatting at you or other pets. They might also start scratching furniture more than usual or knocking things over as a way of releasing pent-up energy. If your cat displays sudden aggression, it's important to approach them with patience and try to determine the root cause.

Excessive grooming is a common stress response in cats. While grooming is a normal and soothing behavior, a stressed cat may overdo it, leading to bald patches or irritated skin. This is known as psychogenic alopecia and is often caused by anxiety. If you notice your cat licking or biting themselves excessively, they may be using grooming as a coping mechanism.

A sudden increase in vocalization, such as excessive meowing, yowling, or growling, can also indicate stress. Some cats become more vocal when they feel anxious or insecure. If your usually quiet cat starts meowing persistently or making unusual sounds, pay attention to their surroundings and recent changes in their routine.

Changes in sleeping patterns are another sign of stress. A stressed cat may sleep more than usual, withdrawing from their environment as a way to cope. Alternatively, they may become restless and struggle to settle down, pacing around or acting on edge. Observing your cat's sleep habits can give you insight into their emotional state.

Body language is a key indicator of stress in cats. A tense body, flattened ears, a puffed-up tail, or dilated pupils all suggest that your cat is feeling anxious. If your cat crouches low to the ground with their tail tucked in, they might be feeling fearful. Purring, while often associated with contentment, can sometimes be a sign of stress, especially if your cat is purring in an unusual situation, such as during a visit to the vet.

Yawning, lip licking, and excessive blinking are subtle signs of stress that are often overlooked. These behaviors are displacement activities, meaning your cat does them to relieve tension when they feel uncomfortable. If you notice these signs in a situation where your cat is normally relaxed, it may indicate they are feeling uneasy.

Your cat's response to stress will depend on their personality and the source of their anxiety. Some cats become more attached and seek comfort, while others withdraw and prefer to be left alone. Identifying and reducing stressors in your cat's environment is crucial to maintaining their mental and physical well-being.

If you suspect your cat is stressed, take steps to create a calm and predictable environment for them. Avoid sudden changes in their routine, provide hiding places where they can feel safe, and ensure they have access to food, water, and a clean litter box in a quiet area. Playing with your cat and engaging them in interactive activities can also help relieve stress by providing mental and physical stimulation.

Stress in cats should never be ignored, as it can lead to serious health problems over time. If your cat's stress symptoms persist despite making environmental adjustments, consult a veterinarian to rule out any underlying medical conditions. With the right care and attention, you can help your cat feel more relaxed and comfortable in their home.

Spotting Early Signs of Illness

Cats are experts at hiding their pain and discomfort, which makes it challenging to detect when something is wrong. In the wild, showing weakness can make an animal vulnerable to predators, and domestic cats still retain this instinct. As a cat owner, it is your responsibility to recognize the early signs of illness before they become severe. Detecting problems early can mean the difference between a minor issue and a life-threatening condition.

Changes in eating habits are often the first indicator of illness. If your cat suddenly refuses to eat or eats significantly less than usual, it could signal a problem. Loss of appetite can be linked to dental issues, digestive problems, infections, or more serious conditions like kidney disease. On the other hand, an increase in appetite, especially in an older cat, can indicate thyroid disease or diabetes. It is important to monitor your cat's eating habits closely and note any unusual patterns.

Drinking more or less water than usual is another key sign. If your cat is suddenly drinking excessive amounts of water, it could be a sign of diabetes, kidney disease, or hyperthyroidism. Conversely, a decrease in water intake can lead to dehydration, which is particularly dangerous for cats. You can check for dehydration by gently pinching the skin on the back of their neck—if it doesn't quickly return to its normal position, your cat may be dehydrated and require immediate attention.

Litter box habits can reveal a lot about your cat's health. If your cat is urinating more frequently, struggling to urinate, or avoiding the litter box, it may indicate a urinary tract infection, bladder stones, or even a life-threatening blockage. Diarrhea or constipation can be caused by dietary changes, stress, parasites, or gastrointestinal diseases. If you notice blood in the stool or urine, a strong odor, or unusual consistency, it is best to consult a veterinarian.

Behavioral changes can also point to illness. If your normally active and playful cat suddenly becomes lethargic and uninterested in their surroundings, this is a sign that they are not feeling well. A cat that hides more than usual, avoids interaction, or becomes unusually aggressive may be experiencing pain or discomfort. A friendly cat that suddenly avoids being touched might have an injury or an internal issue that needs attention.

Unexplained weight loss or gain should never be ignored. A cat losing weight despite eating normally may have an underlying health condition like hyperthyroidism, diabetes, or cancer. Rapid weight gain, especially if the cat is not overeating, could indicate fluid retention caused by heart or liver disease. If you notice changes in your cat's body condition, consult a veterinarian for a thorough check-up.

Vomiting and excessive drooling are common signs of illness. While an occasional hairball is normal, frequent vomiting can indicate problems such as kidney disease, poisoning, gastrointestinal disorders, or infections. If your cat vomits multiple times in a short period, or if the vomit contains blood or bile, seek veterinary care immediately. Excessive drooling can be a sign of dental disease, nausea, or ingestion of toxic substances.

Breathing difficulties require urgent attention. If your cat is breathing heavily, panting, coughing, or making wheezing sounds, they may have a respiratory infection, asthma, or even heart disease. Unlike dogs, cats do not normally pant unless they are extremely stressed or overheated, so any unusual breathing should be treated as a potential emergency.

Coat and skin condition can also reflect your cat's health. A healthy cat's coat is smooth, shiny, and well-groomed. If you notice excessive shedding, bald patches, dandruff, or a greasy or unkempt appearance, it may indicate a skin infection, allergies, or an underlying illness. Cats that stop grooming themselves may be feeling unwell, experiencing arthritis pain, or suffering from stress.

Eye and nose discharge should not be ignored. Watery or cloudy eyes, redness, or persistent blinking can be signs of an eye infection, injury, or respiratory illness. If your cat's nose is runny, crusty, or accompanied by sneezing, they may have an upper respiratory infection. In severe cases, nasal discharge with blood or thick mucus could indicate more serious conditions such as tumors or fungal infections.

Ear problems can cause discomfort and signal an infection. If your cat frequently shakes their head, scratches their ears, or has a foul smell coming from their ears, they may have an ear infection, mites, or allergies. Dark, waxy buildup or discharge inside the ear is another sign of trouble. Left untreated, ear infections can lead to more serious complications, including hearing loss.

Cats can develop dental problems just like humans. Bad breath, swollen gums, drooling, difficulty eating, or pawing at the mouth can be signs of gum disease, tooth decay, or oral infections. Dental issues can cause severe pain and may lead to other health problems if bacteria from the mouth enter the bloodstream. Regular dental care and check-ups can help prevent these issues.

If you notice any of these signs in your cat, do not wait for them to worsen. Cats often mask their discomfort until the illness has progressed, making early detection crucial. Even if a symptom seems minor, it is always better to have it checked out by a veterinarian. Regular health monitoring, a balanced diet, and routine check-ups can help ensure your cat stays happy and healthy for years to come.

When to Visit the Vet

Cats are known for their independence, but that does not mean they do not require medical attention. As a cat owner, you need to be able to distinguish between minor issues that can be monitored at home and situations that require professional veterinary care. Since cats often hide their pain and discomfort, early intervention is crucial in preventing minor health concerns from becoming serious problems. Knowing when to visit the vet can help you provide the best care for your cat and ensure they live a long, healthy life.

Routine veterinary visits are essential, even if your cat appears healthy. Preventative care, such as vaccinations, dental check-ups, and parasite control, can help identify potential health issues before they become severe. Kittens require several vet visits during their first few months for vaccinations and developmental monitoring, while adult cats should have an annual check-up. Senior cats, typically those over seven years old, should visit the vet at least twice a year due to their increased risk of age-related illnesses. During these routine visits, the vet will examine your cat's weight, coat condition, dental health, and organ function, ensuring that any concerns are addressed early.

There are, however, situations where immediate veterinary attention is necessary. Any sudden change in eating habits should not be ignored. If your cat refuses to eat for more than 24 hours, this could indicate a serious problem such as liver disease, dental pain, or gastrointestinal issues. Cats rely on a consistent intake of food, and prolonged fasting can lead to hepatic lipidosis, a life-threatening liver condition. A sudden increase in appetite, especially in older cats, may signal hyperthyroidism or diabetes. Changes in drinking habits, whether excessive thirst or complete avoidance of water, can be a sign of kidney disease, diabetes, or dehydration and should prompt a vet visit.

Litter box habits are another major indicator of health. If your cat is straining to urinate, producing very little urine, or crying out in pain while in the litter box, they may have a urinary tract infection or a blockage, which can be fatal if untreated. Blood in the urine or stool should always be taken seriously, as it could indicate infections, kidney disease, or even cancer. Frequent diarrhea or constipation that lasts more than 48 hours also requires veterinary attention, as prolonged digestive issues can lead to severe dehydration and other complications.

Vomiting and excessive drooling can sometimes occur due to minor issues like hairballs or mild stomach upset. However, frequent vomiting, vomiting with blood, or vomiting accompanied by lethargy and loss of appetite can indicate poisoning, infections, or serious digestive problems. Similarly, excessive drooling, difficulty swallowing, or bad breath can be signs of dental disease, mouth infections, or even ingestion of toxic substances. If your cat exhibits these symptoms, a vet visit is necessary to determine the cause.

Difficulty breathing is always an emergency. If your cat is panting, wheezing, coughing persistently, or breathing with an open mouth, this could be a sign of respiratory infections, asthma, heart disease, or fluid buildup in the lungs. Since breathing problems can escalate quickly, immediate veterinary care is essential.

Behavioral changes are another red flag. If your normally affectionate and active cat becomes withdrawn, hides excessively, or avoids social interaction, they may be experiencing pain or discomfort. Sudden aggression, excessive grooming leading to bald spots, or unusual vocalizations can also indicate stress, illness, or neurological issues. A change in activity levels, such as extreme lethargy or excessive hyperactivity, may signal underlying medical conditions.

Visible injuries or swelling should not be ignored. If your cat has an open wound, limps, or shows signs of pain when touched, they may have an injury or infection that needs medical attention. Swollen areas, especially around the face, limbs, or abdomen, can be signs of abscesses, tumors, or internal injuries. In cases of trauma, such as falling from a height or being hit by a car, even if your cat appears fine, internal injuries may not be immediately visible, making a vet visit essential.

Seizures, disorientation, or sudden loss of balance are serious neurological symptoms that require emergency care. If your cat has a seizure, collapses, or displays confusion and difficulty walking, they may have a neurological disorder, poisoning, or other serious conditions that need immediate diagnosis and treatment.

Eye and ear issues should also be addressed promptly. If your cat has red, swollen, or watery eyes, they may have an infection, injury, or even a more serious condition like glaucoma. Cloudiness or sudden blindness should be treated as an emergency. Similarly, if your cat frequently shakes their head, scratches their ears, or has a foul smell from the ears, they may have an infection or ear mites. Left untreated, ear infections can cause long-term damage to hearing.

Regular veterinary care is the best way to keep your cat healthy, but knowing when to seek emergency treatment is just as important. Never ignore symptoms that persist or worsen over time. If you are unsure whether your cat needs medical attention, it is always better to err on the side of caution and consult a veterinarian. Early diagnosis and treatment can save your cat's life and prevent unnecessary suffering.

Parting Words on Chapter

Understanding the signs of stress and illness in cats allows for early intervention, preventing minor issues from escalating into serious conditions. Observing behavioral and physical changes closely ensures timely veterinary care, promoting a healthier, longer life for feline companions.

CHAPTER 10: CAT ENRICHMENT AND PLAY

Cat enrichment and play involve activities that stimulate a cat's mind and body, ensuring a healthy and fulfilling life. These elements are essential in preventing boredom, reducing stress, and encouraging natural behaviors such as hunting, climbing, and exploring. A well-enriched environment enhances a cat's physical health, sharpens cognitive abilities, and strengthens bonds with its owner. Lack of stimulation can lead to anxiety, obesity, and destructive behaviors. Understanding the importance of play and mental engagement helps create a balanced lifestyle, keeping cats active, entertained, and emotionally satisfied. Implementing proper enrichment strategies improves overall well-being and enhances daily life quality.

Importance of Play for Cats

Cats are natural hunters, full of energy and curiosity. Even if your cat spends most of its time lounging around the house, play is an essential part of its well-being. Play is more than just a way for cats to pass the time—it's a critical component of their physical, mental, and emotional health. Engaging in regular playtime helps prevent behavioral issues, reduces stress, and strengthens the bond between you and your feline friend. Understanding why play is important and how to incorporate it into your cat's daily routine can significantly improve its quality of life.

Cats have an instinct to chase, pounce, and explore. In the wild, they rely on these skills to catch food and survive. Even though domestic cats don't need to hunt, their bodies and minds still crave that stimulation. Without play, cats can become bored, anxious, or even destructive. Providing the right amount of play helps maintain their natural instincts while keeping them happy and healthy.

A playful cat is a healthy cat. Regular activity keeps your cat's body in good shape by helping it maintain a healthy weight, improving coordination, and strengthening muscles. Obesity is a major issue among indoor cats, often leading to diabetes, joint pain, and heart disease. When a cat plays, it engages its entire body, from its legs and paws to its spine and tail. Activities like chasing a toy or jumping onto surfaces mimic the movements it would make while hunting, providing a full-body workout. Cats that get enough exercise are more agile and less likely to suffer from mobility problems as they age.

Mental stimulation is just as important as physical exercise. Cats are intelligent creatures that need challenges to stay sharp. Play keeps their minds engaged, preventing boredom and frustration. Without stimulation, a cat might develop behavioral issues such as excessive meowing, scratching furniture, or aggression. Interactive toys that require problem-solving, such as puzzle feeders or treat-dispensing toys, help activate your cat's brain and satisfy its natural curiosity.

Play is also a powerful stress reliever for cats. Many things can cause stress in a cat's life, from a new pet in the house to a change in routine. When a cat plays, it releases built-up energy and tension. This can prevent nervous behaviors such as overgrooming, hiding, or sudden aggression. If your cat seems anxious or withdrawn, introducing more play sessions can help it feel more relaxed and confident.

Beyond health benefits, play strengthens the bond between you and your cat. Unlike dogs, cats are often seen as independent animals, but they still crave social interaction. When you engage in play, you are speaking your cat's language. Using a toy to mimic prey movements makes your cat see you as part of the hunt, creating a shared experience that builds trust.

Many cats that seem aloof or distant may simply need the right kind of interaction to open up. If your cat isn't naturally affectionate, regular playtime might be the key to a closer relationship.

Not all play is the same, and different cats have different preferences. Some enjoy chasing a laser pointer, while others prefer batting at a feather wand or pouncing on a stuffed toy. The key is to experiment and find what excites your cat the most. Rotating toys and introducing new activities regularly keeps things fresh and prevents boredom. However, play should always be safe. Avoid small objects that your cat could swallow, and never use your hands or feet as toys, as this encourages biting and scratching.

The Ideal play session should last around 10 to 15 minutes at a time, at least twice a day. Kittens and young cats usually need more frequent play, while older cats may prefer shorter, gentler sessions. Timing also matters—cats are naturally more active during dawn and dusk, so scheduling play during these hours can feel more natural to them. If your cat suddenly loses interest in playing, it might be a sign of illness or discomfort, so always pay attention to changes in behavior.

Play isn't just about fun—it's a necessity for your cat's well-being. A lack of play can lead to weight gain, stress, and destructive behaviors. A well-stimulated cat is a happy cat, and a happy cat makes for a peaceful home. If you've never made play a priority, now is the time to start. It's never too late to introduce your cat to the joys of active engagement, and the benefits are immediate.

Always supervise play sessions, especially when introducing new toys. Check toys regularly for wear and tear to prevent choking hazards. If using string or ribbon, never leave it unattended, as cats can swallow it, leading to serious digestive issues. Pay attention to your cat's signals—if it seems tired or overstimulated, end the session and let it rest. Lastly, be patient.

Some cats take longer to warm up to play, but with consistency, they will eventually engage.

DIY Toys and Activities

Cats are naturally curious and playful animals, but you don't have to spend a fortune on store-bought toys to keep them entertained. In fact, some of the best toys and activities for cats can be made at home with simple household items. DIY cat toys are not only cost-effective but also allow you to customize play experiences based on your cat's preferences. With a little creativity, you can turn everyday objects into exciting games that provide mental and physical stimulation for your feline friend.

Homemade toys can be just as engaging as store-bought ones, if not more. Many cats prefer simple items like crumpled paper or cardboard boxes over expensive electronic toys. A great example is a basic cardboard box—cats love to jump in, hide, and even pounce from inside them. Cutting holes into the sides of a box and placing small toys inside can create an interactive hide-and-seek game. Adding different-sized boxes together to form a tunnel system adds another level of excitement, encouraging your cat to explore and exercise.

Another easy DIY toy is a paper ball. Crumpling a sheet of paper into a lightweight ball makes a fantastic toy for batting and chasing. Unlike heavier balls, paper is soft and won't damage furniture or make loud noises when thrown around. If your cat enjoys chasing things, you can toss the ball across the floor to mimic prey movement, engaging your cat's hunting instincts.

To make an interactive treat dispenser, you can use an empty toilet paper roll. By cutting small holes into the roll and sealing the ends with paper, you can create a puzzle toy that dispenses treats as your cat bats it around. This stimulates problem-solving skills while also making your cat work for its rewards. Using different-sized treats or kibble pieces can increase the challenge and keep your cat engaged for longer periods.

If your cat enjoys batting at dangling objects, you can create a wand toy using a stick, a piece of string, and a small attachment like a feather or fabric strip. Waving the wand in the air encourages your cat to jump and swat, mimicking the movement of birds or insects. This type of play is excellent for building agility and coordination. However, always store string-based toys away after playtime to prevent your cat from swallowing them.

For a more advanced DIY toy, consider making a sock stuffed with catnip. Take an old sock, fill it with dried catnip, and tie a knot at the end. The scent of catnip excites many cats, leading to playful rolling, rubbing, and pouncing. If your cat doesn't respond to catnip, try using a crinkly material inside the sock to create a sound effect that grabs attention.

Creating a simple obstacle course with household objects can turn playtime into an engaging activity. Using pillows, small chairs, and tunnels made from blankets, you can encourage your cat to jump, crawl, and explore. Hiding treats or toys at different points in the course adds an extra layer of excitement and keeps your cat moving.

If your cat enjoys scratching, a DIY scratching post can be made using a sturdy cardboard tube or wooden post wrapped in sisal rope. Scratching is essential for maintaining healthy claws and stretching muscles. Providing a homemade scratching surface can also protect your furniture from unwanted claw marks.

Some cats love water play, and a simple bowl of water with floating objects, like ping-pong balls or ice cubes, can be a great source of entertainment. Watching your cat paw at the objects as they move across the water stimulates curiosity and coordination. This is especially useful for cats that need extra encouragement to stay active.

DIY toys and activities allow you to bond with your cat while ensuring it gets the exercise and mental stimulation it needs. By experimenting with different materials and play styles, you can discover what excites your cat the most.

Changing the toys regularly keeps things interesting and prevents boredom. Playtime is not only about fun—it's essential for a cat's well-being, reducing stress, preventing obesity, and strengthening your relationship.

Always monitor your cat when introducing new toys, especially those made with fabric, string, or small parts that could be swallowed. Check toys regularly for wear and tear, discarding any that could pose a choking hazard. If your cat loses interest in a toy, rotate it out of sight for a few days before reintroducing it. Avoid using household items that contain toxic substances, such as plastic bags or materials with sharp edges. Play should always be safe and enjoyable.

Keeping Your Cat Mentally Stimulated

Cats are naturally intelligent and curious animals, and just like humans, they need mental stimulation to stay happy and healthy. A bored cat is more likely to develop behavioral problems such as excessive meowing, scratching furniture, or even aggression. Mental stimulation is just as important as physical exercise, helping to keep your cat engaged and preventing stress-related issues. By introducing activities that challenge your cat's mind, you can ensure that it remains sharp, active, and content.

One of the easiest ways to keep your cat mentally stimulated is through interactive play. Cats are natural hunters, and their instincts drive them to stalk, chase, and pounce. Using toys that mimic prey, such as feather wands, toy mice, or laser pointers, encourages this behavior and provides a satisfying challenge. Rotating toys regularly prevents boredom and keeps your cat interested in play. If your cat seems uninterested in a toy, putting it away for a few days and reintroducing it later can renew its excitement.

Puzzle feeders and treat-dispensing toys are excellent for engaging a cat's problem-solving skills. Instead of simply placing food in a bowl, using a feeder that requires your cat to work for its food encourages natural foraging behavior. You can create a simple puzzle feeder by cutting holes into a cardboard box and placing treats inside, making your cat figure out how to get them. Store-bought puzzle feeders come in various difficulty levels, allowing you to adjust the challenge based on your cat's experience.

Creating an enriching environment at home is another way to keep your cat's mind active. Cats love to explore, so providing different levels of vertical space, such as cat trees, shelves, or window perches, allows them to climb and observe their surroundings. Placing a perch near a window lets your cat watch birds, cars, and people outside, adding a natural source of entertainment. Bird feeders positioned near a window can provide endless fascination for indoor cats.

Scent enrichment can also stimulate a cat's mind. Introducing new scents, such as catnip, silvervine, or even natural scents from outside, can spark curiosity. Placing a small amount of catnip in different areas of the house or rubbing a towel on plants outside and bringing it in for your cat to sniff can provide a new sensory experience. Some cats enjoy the smell of certain herbs, like chamomile or valerian root, which can have calming effects.

Training sessions offer another excellent way to engage your cat mentally. While many people think of training as something only for dogs, cats are very capable of learning tricks and commands. Using positive reinforcement, such as treats or praise, you can teach your cat to sit, high-five, or even fetch. Training strengthens the bond between you and your cat while also providing a rewarding mental challenge. Clicker training, in which a small clicking device signals correct behavior followed by a reward, Is particularly effective for teaching cats new skills.

Social interaction is a crucial part of mental stimulation. While cats are often independent, they still need regular engagement with their owners. Talking to your cat, petting it, and playing interactive games create a strong emotional connection. Some cats enjoy supervised outdoor time, which can be achieved by training them to walk on a leash or providing a secure outdoor enclosure. Experiencing new sights, sounds, and smells outside adds an extra layer of enrichment to their daily routine.

Introducing new objects and textures into your cat's environment prevents monotony. Rotating furniture arrangements, adding new scratching posts, or even placing paper bags or cardboard boxes around the house creates new opportunities for exploration. Many cats enjoy hiding and pouncing out of boxes or crawling through tunnels. Something as simple as changing the placement of familiar objects can make a space feel new and exciting to a cat.

Companion animals can also play a role in mental stimulation. Some cats enjoy the company of another cat or even a well-behaved dog. If you are considering adding another pet to the household, a slow and careful introduction is essential to ensure a positive relationship. While some cats thrive in multi-pet households, others may prefer being the only pet, so it's important to observe your cat's comfort level.

Keeping your cat mentally stimulated is an ongoing process that requires variety and creativity. Engaging your cat in daily activities that challenge its mind reduces stress, prevents destructive behavior, and enhances overall well-being. A stimulated cat is a happy cat, and a happy cat makes for a peaceful and enjoyable home environment.

Always monitor your cat's reaction to new activities. While mental challenges are beneficial, overstimulation can lead to frustration. If your cat seems uninterested or agitated, try a different approach or reduce the level of difficulty. Be patient, as some cats take longer to adapt to new forms of stimulation. Avoid forcing interactions or using overwhelming sensory experiences, as this can create anxiety rather than enrichment. Finding the right balance ensures your cat remains both mentally and emotionally content.

Parting Words on Chapter

A well-enriched cat is a happy and well-behaved companion. Play and mental stimulation prevent behavioral issues, improve health, and strengthen bonds. Regularly introducing new activities keeps curiosity alive, ensuring a fulfilling and balanced life that meets both physical and psychological needs.

CONCLUSION

A well-enriched cat leads a healthier, happier life. Physical activity, mental stimulation, and interactive engagement prevent stress, boredom, and behavioral issues. Understanding a cat's instincts allows for better companionship, fostering trust and emotional well-being. Simple play routines, DIY toys, and structured activities create a fulfilling environment that supports both physical and psychological needs. Commitment to enrichment strengthens the human-cat bond, ensuring a rewarding and harmonious relationship. Small, consistent efforts lead to a more active, content, and well-adjusted feline companion.

Made in the USA
Coppell, TX
02 July 2025

51377571R20128